Backpacking
Overnights

North Carolina Mountains • South Carolina Upstate

Jim Parham

**milestone
press**

almond, nc

Milestone Press, P.O. Box 158, Almond, NC 28702
www.milestonepress.com

Cover design by Martha Smith Design
Book design by Denise Gibson/Design Den www.designden.com
  & Jim Parham
Cover photographs by Jim Parham (front) & Mary Ellen Hammond (back).
All interior photographs are by the author unless otherwise indicated.

Library of Congress Cataloging-in-Publication Data

Parham, Jim.
  Backpacking overnights : North Carolina mountains, South Carolina
upstate / Jim Parham.
      pages cm
   Summary: "Lists fifty overnight backpacking excursions in the mountains of North Carolina and South Carolina, with maps, hiking and
driving directions, and backcountry campsite locations. Destinations
include Great Smoky Mountains National Park, Pisgah and Nantahala
National Forests, Linville Gorge Wilderness, and more. Includes information on choosing and using backpacking gear; trail etiquette; and
selecting a route"--Provided by publisher.
   ISBN 978-1-889596-28-0 (alk.paper)
   1. Backpacking--North Carolina---Guidebooks. 2. Backpacking--
South Carolina--Guidebooks. 3. North Carolina--Guidebooks. 4.
South Carolina--Guidebooks. I. Title.
   GV199.42.N66P37 2013
   796.510975--dc23
                          2013002166

Printed in the United States on recycled paper

The Spirit of Adventure

Take a look at the photos as you flip through this book. You'll notice that many show youngsters out enjoying time on the trail. There is a reason for this. The mountains of North and South Carolina are home to around 100 summer youth camps, one of the largest concentrations of camps in the United States. Given the beauty of the southern Appalachians and the abundance of national parks and forests, it's no wonder. Most any day from early June through mid-August you are likely to meet a group of young campers in the backcountry—splashing in the stream at Pisgah's Sliding Rock, rolling along on mountain bikes in the Nantahala National Forest, paddling canoes and kayaks on South Carolina's Chattooga River, rock climbing in the Panthertown Valley, or backpacking along the Appalachian Trail. For some it's their first outing, and many will continue to seek outdoor experiences into adulthood.

For years now I have had the privilege of leading outdoor adventure groups for Falling Creek Camp for Boys in Tuxedo, North Carolina. The camp has a top-notch adventure program, offering a great learning experience for everyone involved. In the backpacking program, boys learn to pack their own packs, cook their own meals, set up their own campsite, work as a team, find their way along a trail, and many other essential outdoor skills. In turn, I've learned about reasonable daily hiking distances for different ability levels, what makes an overnight hike spectacular or just so-so, which gear holds up to daily use and abuse and which does not, how to keep smiling when it's pouring rain and everyone is soaked through, and just how important it is that the knowledge and spirit of adventure be passed from one generation to the next.

In this era of virtual reality and electronic everything, exposing youngsters to the independence of outdoor adventure is as important as ever. For many kids, a person who can walk out in the woods and spend the night there is pretty cool. If you do that, they'll want to be like you. So, for the youth in your life, be a backpacker (kayaker, mountain biker), and let them know how much you enjoy it.

Table of Contents

Nantahala National Forest
Joyce Kilmer–Slickrock Wilderness Area
Nantahala River Area
Standing Indian Area
Highlands Plateau Area

Table of Contents (cont.)

South Carolina Upstate

SC State Parks & Mountain Bridge Wilderness

Chattooga National Wild & Scenic River

Appendices

Introduction

Backpacking is more than just going for a long walk in the woods. You're carrying on your back everything you need to survive in comfort for a night, a weekend, or many days at a time. It's an experience in which your world very quickly becomes you, your hiking companions, and the backcountry. As in the version of *Big Rock Candy Mountain* that my dad used to sing—*I'm going to a land where everything's bright; I'll hang my clothes on a hickory limb, and sleep out every night*—it's simple and carefree. Plus, a night out on the trail is awesome. The day users have gone home, and you've got the woods to yourself. You'll be there for sunset and sunrise. Foods that would be mediocre at home taste delicious. You cozy up to a campfire with a hot drink in your hands. And finding your campsite is like getting to pick a new home every day.

The mountains of western North Carolina and upstate South Carolina are part of the southern Appalachian chain that stretches from Georgia north to Maine. In North Carolina these mountains rise to peaks well over 6,000 feet, the highest in the East, in ranges called the Nantahalas, the Balsams, the Blacks, and the most famous of all, the Great Smokies. It's a land of national forests and national parks. Upstate South Carolina is famous for what the Cherokees called the "blue wall." Just below the border with North Carolina, the Blue Ridge Escarpment rises up out of the piedmont, and the National Wild and Scenic Chattooga River flows down out of the hills.

These mountains are dotted with public land crisscrossed with thousands of miles of designated hiking trails, and it's great backpacking territory. You'll find the trails well marked with easy-to-find trailheads, good campsites, and water from free-flowing, clear mountain streams. You might spend a night out beside a waterfall, in a shelter on the Appalachian Trail, or on a ridge where you can watch the sunrise from your sleeping bag.

The aim of this book is to provide all the information you need to find the best overnight backpacking destinations. Some routes are relatively easy—perfect for first-timers or those who have time only for an overnight. A two-mile hike out to a campsite beside the river may be just your thing. If you're a seasoned veteran, there's plenty to choose from as well. You might want a strenuous challenge, hiking 20 miles in two days or following routes over steep terrain, or both. The majority of routes listed here fall somewhere in between, and each has at least one special destination—a waterfall, a high-mountain bog, a lookout tower, scenic riverbanks, an open bald, or an old homesite to explore.

Newcomers to backpacking will find the front of this book particularly helpful. If choosing gear, packing a pack, cooking on a camp stove, or learning how to hike with a 25-pound load seems daunting, the guidelines and suggestions in this section should put you well on your way to a feeling of backcountry confidence. Even those who've spent a considerable amount of time on the trail may find useful information here.

When's the best time of year for backpacking in the North and South Carolina mountains? It's a matter of personal preference. Summers can get hot, especially in the lower elevations, but you'll carry less in your pack. More folks are on the trail, so go early on a weekend or head out in the middle of the week to be sure you'll find a campsite. Winter is the opposite, with colder nights, especially in the higher elevations, and shorter days. You'll need a beefy tent, a good sleeping bag, and plenty of warm clothes. All that bulk adds weight, but your reward will be solitude.

In spring and fall, days and nights alike are often clear and pleasant. Appalachian springtime is famous for wildflower displays. After the dreariness of winter, time in the bright green woods will make you feel alive. Fall is when all those green leaves turn red, yellow, and orange before they come tumbling down. The weather can be brilliant—nature's swan song before winter settles in.

No matter when you go, backpacking in the Carolina mountains is a fantastic adventure. Gather the information you need from this guide, then hit the trail in one of the most beautiful places on earth.

Preparing for Your Trip

Gear Checklist

Nothing can ruin a good hike quicker than leaving something essential behind. Remember the Scout motto? Be prepared. Here's a checklist of items for an overnight hike.

To Carry
- backpack
- sleeping bag
- sleeping pad
- shelter
- stove & fuel, with matches or lighter
- cook pot(s)
- food
- food storage system
- eating utensils
- water container
- water purification system
- headlamp or flashlight
- pocket knife
- first aid kit
- map/guidebook
- extra clothes (see *To Wear*, below)
- large, heavy-duty plastic bag

Optional
- trekking poles
- pack cover
- camera

- phone
- GPS
- camp chair
- bandana
- insect repellent
- backpack repair kit

To Wear (this is your base layer; no cotton anything)
- footwear
- synthetic or woolen-blend hiking socks
- shorts or light pants
- quick-dry t-shirt (woolen or synthetic)
- cap or wide-brimmed hat

Add
- long-sleeved synthetic shirt
- fleece or wind shirt
- rain jacket & pants
- light gloves
- warm hat

Optional
- Sunglasses
- neon or bright orange vest (hunting season)

Choosing and Using Your Gear

When it comes to outdoor gear, there are so many options to choose from that it can seem overwhelming. You can buy gear online, at brick and mortar outfitter stores, at big discount stores, or at used equipment sales. At a brick and mortar outfitter, the staff is usually trained to fit backpacks and proper footwear, size sleeping bags, and help in other ways. Since you'll likely find yourself shopping elsewhere at times, this section is intended to help simplify the gear acquisition process.

Backpack

A properly fitted backpack is essential to the enjoyment and comfort of an overnight hike. Packs come in two basic types—internal frame and external frame. There are top-notch models in both categories, so choosing between the two boils down to personal preference.

Fit is critical. Packs are designed according to gender and build. How long is your torso? What is your hip size? How do you plan to use the pack? To determine your torso length, measure your back from the bony knob at the base of your neck (cervical vertebra 7) to an imaginary horizontal line across the top of your hip bones. Each pack specifies a torso length and whether it's designed for a man or a woman. A good pack also comes with a hip belt, which is why you also need your hip size. For that, measure around the top of your pelvis, where the hip belt will rest.

A properly fitted and loaded pack just looks right.

Sizes range from x-small to large, depending on how you plan to use your pack. Keep in mind that space provided usually equals space filled. If you end up with a high-capacity pack, chances are you're going to fill it up with gear whether you really need it all or not. The end result will have you lugging a pack that's cumbersome and much too heavy. So, be practical. On overnight or weekend hikes during the warmer months you can get away with a pack as small as 35 liters, and unless you're heading out on a major expedition it's rare to need one larger than 60 liters. Somewhere in between will probably meet your needs, and remember—you're not required to fill it.

Sleeping Bag

A comfortable, lightweight, easy-to-pack sleeping bag is a must. You don't want to spend a teeth-chattering night waiting for daylight, nor do you want to lug a bag that takes up 90 percent of your pack space. Make sure you have a decent bag. Here's how to choose.

Length is important if you're tall. Bags come in regular (6 feet or shorter) and long (more than 6 feet).

Rating refers to temperature. Zero-degree, 15-degree, 25-degree, 60-degree are all comfort levels. A 25-degree bag will keep the average person warm to 25°F. If you tend to get cold easily, don't count on it. Some bags will also list their "extreme" ratings. A bag with extreme rating 35°F will not keep you comfortably warm at 35 degrees, but it will keep you alive.

Shape choices are mummy (body-shaped), tapered, and rectangular. A mummy bag will be more versatile. It has a hood (for warmth) and typically packs up light.

Fill for sleeping bags is down, synthetic, or cotton. Steer clear of cotton; it's too heavy and bulky, but sometimes choosing between down and synthetic is tough. Down bags are generally more expensive and lighter, pack up smaller, and (like cotton), are useless when wet. Top-notch synthetic bags can pack up nearly as small, are not quite as light as down, often cost less, and can still keep you warm when wet.

Sleeping Pad

For backpacking, there are three basic types of sleeping pads available: air pads, self-inflating pads, and closed-cell foam.

Air pads have either all air or air plus insulating material between you and the ground. Usually they are lightweight and pack up pretty small. However, they are not warming in cool weather, and if the air leaks out overnight, there's essentially nothing between you and the hard ground.

Self-inflating pads incorporate the best of an air pad and a foam pad and are usually the most expensive choice. Don't expect them to completely self-inflate; you still have to top them off. Should they leak, you're left with a little padding. They are also the warmest choice.

Closed-cell foam pads are light but bulky, and they are inexpensive. Most people carry them on the outside of their pack. They do an adequate job of padding and can double as lightning protection in a thunderstorm (see *Safety*, p. 36).

Shelter

It's rare in the Carolina mountains to be able to sleep under the stars without waking up wet, even if it doesn't rain. With the relatively high humidity in the southern Appalachians, at some point during the night the atmosphere will reach what is known as the dew point. When this happens, everything exposed to the heavens above will suddenly have a layer of moisture on it (when it's cold enough, this moisture becomes frost). For this reason, most folks carry their own shelter. Here are the options.

Tarps are the simplest, lightest, and least expensive way to go (see *Going Light,* p. 20), but not everyone likes the feeling of an open-ended structure. Tarps don't trap heat as tents do. Bugs can buzz in, plus there's not that fully enclosing micro-thin piece of nylon to keep the bears away.

Lightweight backpacking tents provide more protection. Don't skimp too much here; those cheap big box store models are heavy, hard to set up, and collapse in the first big storm. Unless you plan to camp on the flanks of Mt. Mitchell in January, you'll be happy with a three-season model. Look for one as small as you think you can stand. You'll appreciate its lightness while you're carrying it more than you'll notice its small size when you're asleep.

Hanging out in a hammock can feel luxurious in a campsite.

Backpacking hammocks combine the simplicity of a nylon tarp (you'll still need one to cover the hammock) with the coziness of a tent. Most nylon hammocks can be pulled around you like a cocoon, keeping out bugs and most other critters. In summer you can leave the ground cloth and sleeping pad at home; you don't need level ground, but you do need two trees a certain distance apart to set it up. No matter what the temperature rating of your sleeping bag, in cooler weather you'll want your sleeping pad in the hammock with you for warmth.

Trail shelters are provided on some of the routes listed in this book. Most of these are three-sided, open on the front with a wooden floor. Some have wooden bunks or sleeping platforms. If you plan to use a trail shelter, always bring along some alternative—a tent, or at least a tarp; nothing can be worse than arriving late to a shelter and finding it full. Be aware that shelters are favorite homes for mice. Heavy use can attract other critters, too, so protect your food and your pack. Since mice can climb ropes, a common method is to hang your pack inside the shelter with some type of barrier on the rope between the pack and whatever it is tied to. At some shelters, hikers have left ropes with empty tuna cans suspended in the middle for this very purpose.

Cooking System

Overnight backpacking requires carrying food for multiple meals. Some food will require cooking or at the very least hot water for rehydration. For this you'll want some sort of lightweight back-packing stove, a cook pot or two, something from which to eat, and a utensil to get it to your mouth. Stoves come in dozens of models; choosing the best one for you is a matter of personal preference. Unless you plan to feed an army, you can get by just fine with a single one-burner. Look for something that packs up small with an easy fuel system. Most of your

You can make a super-light alcohol stove from a soda can.

choices will use either canister or liquid fuel.

Canister fuel stoves are easiest to use. Just screw on the canister, turn the dial, and light. You can't normally refill the canister, and not all canisters are alike, so you may have difficulty finding fuel. They are not as effec-tive in cold weather.

Liquid fuel stoves are generally more expensive and can be finicky. However, many burn various types of fuel (white gas, diesel, kerosene), and they work well in all weather. (See *Going Light,* p. 20, for information on alcohol stoves.)

Pots and Utensils should be minimal. If you're going solo, there's no need to bring more than one small lidded pot that holds about a quart; you can eat straight from the pot. Rarely will you need more than just a bowl, mug, and spoon/spork. Also handy is a small scrubbing pad. With that and water, you can get most anything clean enough for the next meal or until you get home.

Water Container

Generally your water container is a water bottle, but more and more people are using hydration bladders these days as well. Whichever you choose, you'll want to have the capacity to carry about two liters.

Bottles come in plastic and lightweight stainless steel. While a plastic water, juice, or soda bottle works in a pinch, purchasing a more durable bottle made for reuse is best.

Hydration bladders are bag-like containers of heavy duty plastic with a drinking tube attached. The bladder fits in your pack, which may have a special sleeve for it and a port for the tube to run through. Bladders are great for keeping you hydrated; just bite down on the valve at the end of the tube to release water into your mouth while you're hiking along. It's a good idea to have a water bottle in addition to a water bladder; it's useful to have in camp, and it's risky to rely solely on a bladder that could get punctured, a tube that could clog, and a bite valve that could malfunction.

Water Purification System

You need a plan for making sure you have water that's safe to drink. No matter how clear the water in the stream looks, chances are there may be something in it that could make you sick. So, you have three choices—you can treat it, filter it, or boil it.

Purification tablets contain chemicals that kill any and all bugs living in the water. Usually you just drop in a tablet, and wait 30 minutes or so. This is the simplest and least expensive water purification method, but it leaves your water with a taste you might not enjoy. Fairly new to the market is a gadget that treats water with ultraviolet radiation. It looks like a little flashlight and blasts your water with UV rays, killing all the bugs. These are fast, effective, and cost about the same as a hand-pumped filter. They also use batteries. You'll need spares, since the rig is useless without them.

Filters come in various makes and models. All incorporate some way of forcing the water through a ceramic filter that removes contaminants. Your water comes out clean, clear, and tastes like water. Except for the time it takes to work the pump, there is no waiting. A filter is usually the most expensive option, and it takes up the most space in your pack.

Pumping water through a filter is one way to purify it.

Boiling is the most basic purification method. Three minutes at a rolling boil and you've killed all the bad stuff. Sounds simple and cheap, right? Boiling enough to keep you hydrated takes time and uses a lot of expensive fuel, so don't use it for drinking water. However, it is perfectly acceptable to draw water straight from the stream to boil for cooking or making hot drinks. As long as what you're making calls for *boiling* water, you're good. But don't make the mistake of just getting the water hot so you can rehydrate a meal. If you do, all those bugs will just keep on swimming right into your supper. Unless it's boiled, make sure your hot water is first treated or filtered.

Lights

This one is fairly straightforward. You'll need to carry something that lets you see in the dark. Not so long ago, most folks used a **flashlight**, and there are still a variety of small models out there to choose from. The best choice, though, is a **headlamp**. A headlamp leaves your hands free to do whatever, and always points where you are looking. Go for a lightweight one that will stay securely on your head.

Food Storage System

While out in the woods, you'll need some way to protect your food. *Hanging a bear bag* is the most common method. Put everything into a nylon or plastic bag—all your food, anything that might have remnants of food on it (pot, bowl, spoon) or might smell like food (toothpaste, lip balm). Hang this bag from a tree so bears, raccoons, possums, mice, squirrels, friendly dog from the next campsite, or any other critter can't get to it. You'll need a small-diameter rope around 30 feet long (parachute cord works well), a small carabiner, and preferably a nylon bag large enough to hold all your food-related items. Suspend the bag at least 10 feet off the ground and at least 4 feet from the nearest tree or branch. Finding a suitable tree (or trees) for this purpose is one of the first things you should do once in your campsite; definitely don't wait until after dark. All campsites and shelters in the Great Smoky Mountains

Some campsites have bear cable rigs set up for your use.

National Park have a special cable system for hanging bear bags. *Bearproof canisters* are another option. In some places in the western United States these are required. If you plan to camp in a treeless area, they are critical. They are light and easier to use than a bear bag, but they are also big, bulky, and not much fun when stuffing in your pack.

First Aid Kit

Accidents on the trail do happen, and you should be ready to deal with them. (see *Safety*, p. 32). Having some form of first aid kit and knowing how to use its contents is part of being a responsible outdoorsperson. There are various preassembled and ready-to-use kits on the market, or you can make up your own. For simple overnight hikes you should be okay with a relatively basic kit.

Contents should include something for cleaning up and bandaging minor cuts or burns, something for blisters (moleskin), something for insect bites (are you allergic?), something for pain and/or swelling, and something to help wrap a strain or sprain. Also know that one seemingly small injury can wipe out an entire kit, so have extra supplies on hand and restock after your trip.

Trekking Poles

This book lists trekking poles as optional. Certainly you can hike without them, and many folks do. However, if you want to save your knees for many years of hiking to come; are planning a trip that includes lots of rocky, rooty, steep terrain; or are "going light" (see p. 20), you'll want to get a pair and learn how to use them. Humans have been using hiking staffs or walking sticks nearly as long as we've been walking upright, and though a single walking stick is useful, trekking poles are vastly superior. At first glance they look like ski poles. They have a nylon or leather loop to fit around your wrist, are usually made of lightweight, hollow metal alloy, and are typically collapsible and adjustable.

Grip them by first sliding your hand through the loop and then clasping the grip so that the loop rests against your palm between your thumb and index finger and between your hand and the grip. Hold the pole loosely, letting your hand hang in the strap.

Fit depends on adjusting the pole length so that at rest your arm is bent comfortably at a right angle.

Technique for walking on level ground or going uphill: the poles should angle slightly back behind you at all times. Push off the ground lightly with each step forward, either alternating right and left while naturally swinging your arms, or double-poling by pushing off both at the same time. Walking downhill, move the poles out in front of you so that as you descend, they take some (but not all) of your

Get the most out of your poles by using the correct grip.

Going Light

Take a trip to Maine's Baxter State Park in August and spend some time at the base of Mt. Katadyn or travel down to Georgia's Springer Mountain in November, and you'll see some of the most experienced backpackers in the world. They'll be on their final leg of completing the 2,184-mile Appalachian Trail. Some went north and some went south, and they've been on the trail for six months. Take a look at their clothing and gear.

Many will wear trail running shoes. Their packs will look like large daypacks. They'll be moving quickly and effortlessly, as if out for a stroll in the park. They won't look anything like the models you see in the outdoor gear catalogs. After months on the trail, they've figured out what they need and what they don't. They know that at the end of a day spent in lightweight shoes their legs are not nearly so tired, and with light packs, the extra support of a heavy boot is not necessary.

They're carrying only what they need, and what they *are* carrying is the smallest and lightest of what they need. They've learned that going light also means avoiding injuries. Many are young and on a tight budget. Instead of a super-expensive, lightweight tent, more than likely they've got a tiny tarp and a scrap of nearly weightless Tyvek® for a ground cloth. Their trekking poles serve double duty as tarp poles. They may be sleeping on a piece of closed-cell foam they've cut down to three quarters of the length of their body. It's also their camp "chair" (see p. 21) and lightning protector (see p.35).

Is their cook stove the latest-greatest in lightweight innovation? Could be, but more than likely they made it themselves from a nearly weightless soda can, and they use an alcohol-based fuel they bought cheaply at an auto parts store. A few dollars worth will last them several weeks. Most of their meals require heating only water. For food, many will buy inexpensive ingredients from regular grocery stores as they go to supplement meals they prepared themselves months before their trip (see *Freezer Bag Cooking*, p. 31) and mailed ahead to be picked up along the way.

Experienced backpackers are experts at layering, making clothes serve double duty whenever possible. Take a whiff. By the smell, you'll know they're probably not carrying too many extras. Sleeping bag? They won't skimp here. It'll be light, warm, and pack up small. Water—that's heavy right? They've learned they can carry a little less water if they drink heavily (like a camel) before leaving camp and each time they fill their container. When all is said and done, their packs may weigh less than twenty pounds. So if you think backpacking means lugging a heavy load of expensive outdoor gear up and down mountains, think again. You can go light, too—and it's especially easy on an overnight trip.

weight, reducing the pressure on your knee joints while providing stability. When moving through very rough terrain, crossing log bridges, and other such places where it might be awkward to use poles, remove the straps from your wrists and carry both poles in one hand.

Camp Chair

You might wonder why another piece of gear initially listed as optional is listed here. A few manufacturers make a soft, hinged "chair" that can be unclipped to lie flat like a sleeping pad. This piece of gear serves many different functions and is well worth carrying along. As a chair, it provides back support and a dry, padded place to sit while eating or hanging out. If you're "going light" (p. 20), it can turn a three-quarter-length sleeping pad into a full length one. If you're sleeping in a hammock and the weather is cooler than you expected, use it to insulate your backside from the cold air. Finally, it's perfect as your lightning pad in an electrical storm (see *Safety*, p. 35). Just strap it to the outside of your pack (some will even roll up), and it's right there when you need it.

Footwear

Most people think that once they decide to go backpacking, they need hiking boots. You've probably heard this before: Buy your boots well ahead of time. Spend days in them and walk miles to make sure they are properly broken in. All good advice, *if you're planning on a major expedition.* Overnight hikes and even trips where you stay out all weekend do not necessarily require purchasing an expensive pair of boots. Especially if you're carrying a lighter pack, a pair of trail runners, low hiking shoes, or lightweight boots will suffice. You may already have

Lightweight hiking boots are comfortable and adequate.

a set of footwear that will do. If you decide to buy something new, trail shoes and light boots take little or no time to break in. If they felt good in the store, they'll probably feel good on the trail. Do they need to be waterproof? Not really. Most folks' feet get wet if it rains hard enough or when they cross a large stream where it's better to keep shoes on (see *Safety*, p. 34). The most important thing is that your footwear fits well, has adequate traction, and is in good condition.

Clothing

Layers. When it comes to clothing you'll need in the backcountry, you should think layers. No matter which layer, always choose wool or synthetic or a blend of the two—*never* cotton.

Base layer consists of socks (should be made for hiking), underwear, a pair of shorts or lightweight long pants, and a quick-dry t-shirt. Again, none of these should be cotton.

Additional layers in any season can include a long-sleeved top that fits fairly snug and packs up small; long underwear or leggings; a lightweight fleece top and/or a featherweight nylon wind shirt, a fleece hat and/or a sun hat, a pair of lightweight gloves, and a rain jacket and pants which double for wind protection. If you're expecting really cold weather, add a few more layers. Throw in a spare pair of socks and underwear, and you should be set. Bringing extra everything may make you feel smug, but chances are it'll be dead weight in your pack. And remember, any clothes you don't sleep in can be stuffed in your sleeping bag stuff sack to make a comfy pillow.

Packing Your Pack

You may wonder how all your gear is going to fit in that little backpack. But if you've planned correctly up to this point, it will. It's all a matter of how you load your pack.

Seek balance—not too top heavy, nor too bottom heavy. As you pack, avoid creating lumps apt to poke you in the back.

Easy access is important. Put items you'll want during the day within easy reach. If you get caught in a rainstorm on the trail, you don't want to have to unload your entire pack to get to your waterproofs. If you have a pack cover (a simple, easily to put on and take off, waterproof nylon "raincoat" for your backpack—very useful), put it in last. Water bottles go in a side pocket where you can reach them without taking off your pack. Ditto your trail map and snacks.

The top pocket (the "brain") of your pack is the safest place for small items like your headlamp, wallet, phone, map or guidebook, and first aid kit. On many models, it can be removed and used as a fanny pack—a very versatile option.

The main compartment—what's the best way to pack it? Remember that big plastic bag from the gear list? Open it out and tuck it down into the hole, pack everything you want to keep dry inside it, then roll or twist the top closed. Whatever you'll want first when you reach your campsite should go in last, toward the top of the main compartment. The things you'll want last (sleeping bag? extra clothes?) should go in first. With experimentation and a few overnights under your belt, you'll find a system that works for you.

Choosing Your Overnight Hike

In general, pick a hike based on your self-assessed ability level and/or your time constraints.

Easier hikes are best for beginners or folks looking for a quick trip out and back. They also make good father-son, mother-daughter, father-daughter (you get the idea) trips.

Moderate routes are for those who have more time or are ready to step up the challenge a notch. Moderately challenging routes make up the bulk of the hikes listed in this book.

Strenuous hikes are for advanced backpackers. Though all the routes listed in this book can be done spending only one night out on the trail, most can just as easily be spread out over two nights or more.

Planning ahead will make your trip infinitely more enjoyable. Does the campsite require an advance reservation—as, for example, in South Carolina state parks or Great Smoky Mountains National Park? How long will it take to reach the trailhead? Have you allowed enough time to get to a campsite well before dark? What's the weather forecast? Are there places where a flooded stream could be difficult or impossible to ford? Consider all these factors when choosing a route.

Leave No Trace: Seven Principles

Plan Ahead and Prepare
- Know the regulations and special concerns for the area you'll visit.
- Prepare for extreme weather, hazards, and emergencies.
- Schedule your trip to avoid times of high use.
- Visit in small groups when possible. Consider splitting larger groups into smaller groups.
- Repackage food to minimize waste.
- Use a map and compass to eliminate the use of marking paint, rock cairns, or flagging.

Travel and Camp on Durable Surfaces
- Durable surfaces include established trails and campsites, rock, gravel, dry grasses, or snow.
- Protect riparian areas by camping at least 200 feet from lakes and streams.
- Good campsites are found, not made. Altering a site is not necessary.

In popular areas:
- Concentrate use on existing trails and campsites.
- Walk single file in the middle of the trail, even when wet or muddy.
- Keep campsites small. Focus activity in areas where vegetation is absent.

In pristine areas:
- Disperse use to prevent the creation of campsites and trails.
- Avoid places where impacts are just beginning.

Dispose of Waste Properly
- Pack it in, pack it out. Inspect your campsite and rest areas for trash or spilled foods. Pack out all trash, leftover food, and litter.
- Deposit solid human waste in catholes dug 6 to 8 inches deep, at least 200 feet from water, camp, and trails. Cover and disguise the cathole when finished.
- Pack out toilet paper and hygiene products.
- To wash yourself or your dishes, carry water 200 feet away from streams or lakes and use small amounts of biodegradable soap. Scatter strained dishwater.

Leave What You Find
- Preserve the past: examine, but do not touch cultural or historic structures and artifacts.
- Leave rocks, plants, and other natural objects as you find them.
- Avoid introducing or transporting non-native species.
- Do not build structures or furniture or dig trenches.

Minimize Campfire Impacts
- Campfires can cause lasting impacts to the backcountry. Use a light-weight stove for cooking and enjoy a candle lantern for light.
- Where fires are permitted, use established fire rings, fire pans, or mound fires.
- Keep fires small. Only use sticks from the ground that can be broken by hand.
- Burn all wood and coals to ash, put out campfires completely, then scatter cool ashes.

Respect Wildlife
- Observe wildlife from a distance. Do not follow or approach them.
- Never feed animals. Feeding wildlife damages their health, alters natural behaviors, and exposes them to predators and other dangers.
- Protect wildlife and your food by storing rations and trash securely.
- Control pets at all times, or leave them at home.
- Avoid wildlife during sensitive times: mating, nesting, raising young, or winter.

Be Considerate of Other Visitors
- Respect other visitors and protect the quality of their experience.
- Be courteous. Yield to other users on the trail.
- Step to the downhill side of the trail when encountering pack stock.
- Take breaks and camp away from trails and other visitors.
- Let nature's sounds prevail. Avoid loud voices and noises.

The member-driven Leave No Trace Center for Outdoor Ethics teaches people how to enjoy the outdoors responsibly. This copyrighted information has been reprinted with permission from the Leave No Trace Center for Outdoor Ethics: www.LNT.org.

On the Trail

How to Hike

It's just walking, right? Yes, but it's not that simple. Carrying a loaded backpack on a rugged mountain trail is vastly different than a tour around the block at home. Negotiating obstacles becomes more complicated. Your pack can snag on branches, and quick hops can turn into slow crawls. Lean too far to one side and you might just topple over, especially if your pack is too heavy or even just top heavy (see *Going Light,* p. 20, and *Packing Your Pack,* p. 22). By the end of the day your step may slow to a plod, and your tired muscles may work differently when fatigued from carrying the extra weight. There's a good chance that after your first trip or two you'll have sore legs, especially if the terrain was hilly. Here are some tips to make your trips easier.

Groups should stay together. The easiest way to achieve this is to have slowest member of the group hike in the front and set the pace.

Trekking poles will help save your knees. For best use, practice makes perfect (see p. 19).

Trail breaks are an important time to rest for a moment and have a snack. Remember, this is supposed to be fun.

Uphills will go more easily if you take shorter steps and land flat-footed for a more efficient stride.

Downhills are a relief, but don't get carried away; you could lose control. Just relax and let gravity help you along. If you're hearing your feet slapping the ground, you'll feel the effects of that later—and not in a good way;

When hiking downhill, relax and let gravity help you along.

you'll have sore feet, knees, and quads. Quiet walking is a sign you're using your entire body more efficiently to absorb the impact.

Trail Etiquette

- Keep other trail users in mind.
- If you're taking a break for more than a few short minutes, move well off the trail.
- If you've found a particularly fine lunch or view spot, don't hog it; other folks will want to stop there as well.
- If you meet equestrian users, give them the right of way.
- Most trail cyclists should give you the right of way; if they don't, step off the trail to let them pass. It's difficult for a mountain biker to get going again on a steep hill, so they'll appreciate your consideration. Remember, most times you'll hear them coming before they see you.
- You're bound to meet other hikers. If you're being overtaken, step off the trail when you can. If you're overtaking someone else, by all means let them know you're back there before you pass, to avoid startling them.
- Generally, communication is the key with all groups. A bit of friendly conversation lets horses know you're human (and their riders know you are educated), cyclists know you care, and fellow hikers know you're there.

Finding, Choosing, and Setting Up Your Campsite

On most routes in this book, rarely will you (nor should you) camp where no one has camped before. Using established campsites is one way to minimize your impact on the environment. Though many of the campsites may be worn, at least you're restricting the wear to one area instead of spreading the damage to any bit of flat ground near a water source.

In the Great Smoky Mountains National Park and South Carolina state parks you'll make a reservation in advance, so once there, what you see is what you get. Everywhere else you'll have a choice, and it's good to know what to look for. A good site will have these elements:

- A water source nearby
- Enough level space to set up your shelter and prepare your food
- An established fire ring, if you plan to have a campfire
- A tree within about 100 yards to hang your bear bag (see p. 18)
- A clean and not completely worn out tent spot
- Protection from open ridgetops where lightning could strike. Also, be wary of standing dead trees within range of your sleeping area; the tree could fall or drop limbs unexpectedly.

Toilet Needs

Most folks can only go so long without having to do number one or number two. Out for overnight, chances are at some point you're going to need to do one, the other, or both. Entire books have been written on this subject, but really it's not too complicated. As long as you're out of sight and away from a water source, number one is pretty straight forward. Going often lets you know you're hydrated.

Technique for number two requires a little more planning. For this, you'll need to get well off the trail, away from camp (if you can see it or hear it, you're too close), and/or at least 200 feet from any water source. Try to pick a pleasant, somewhat hidden place that sees little use. Some people like to hang onto a tree for stability, others hang it over a log, still others just plain squat. Whatever you choose, first scratch out a six- to eight-inch-deep hole (you may want to bring a small plastic hand trowel for this), aim, and fire. That's the first part.

Cleanup is as important as location, so you want to plan ahead. Are you a leaf person or a paper person? If you're a leaf-user, remember to pick some nice big "just right" leaves while you search for your perfect spot. Use them as you would paper and then cover up the whole thing, being careful not to get any on your trowel. If you use paper, the cleanup procedure is a bit more complicated. You'll still cover up your business with the dirt and leaves you scratched aside, but remember the Leave No Trace principles (p. 24): the toilet paper gets packed out. No one likes seeing bright white toilet paper strewn through the woods, and animals do come along and scatter things about. Be sure to carry several plastic zip-top bags for this purpose.

Three Knots You Should Know

You'll use rope in many ways, both on the trail and in the campsite. Being able to tie certain knots will make your life much easier and increase your confidence as a backpacker. Entire books are devoted to this subject and they are a great resource. Learn the three knots outlined here, and you should be able to handle most any situation on your trip.

Clove hitch is used for securing a rope firmly to an object. You might use it to tie one end of a rope to a tree when setting up a tarp, attach a weighted object to one end of the rope to throw a line over a limb, or secure a new strap to your trekking pole should one break.

Clove hitch

Bowline

Bowline is used to make a fixed loop at the end of a rope. You may use a bowline to slip over one end of a tent pole when raising your tent, to attach a carabiner when hanging your bear bag, or to cinch your sleeping pad to your pack.

Taut-line hitch forms a loop that slips in one direction yet holds in the other and allows you to increase the tension easily. Use it to attach the lines on your tent fly to their individual stakes. Once you loop the loose end of line around the stake, you connect the rope to itself with a taut-line

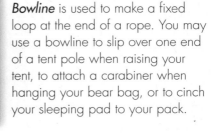

Taut-line hitch

hitch, forming a loop that slides toward the stake to loosen or toward the tarp to tighten. Once tight, it stays securely in place.

Campfires

As long as there is no fire ban in force, campfires can be an enjoyable experience. Cozying up to a crackling fire with only the night sounds and the ruddy flames to keep you company is relatively safe in the southern Appalachian backcountry as long as you follow certain guidelines. *Use existing fire rings* to contain your fire in one area. Most every campsite you come upon will have one fashioned out of

Fire rings keep the fire contained.

rocks. In some parks, there are rings constructed of metal.

Firewood should be dead and down wood only. Don't break down standing dead wood, and never cut down living trees or break off living limbs. In popular campsites, you may have trouble collecting wood for a fire since the nearby area has been scoured by those who've come before you.

Keep fires small to minimize the amount of wood used and increase your safety level. Giant bonfires have their places, but the backcountry is not one of them.

Kill your campfire before leaving your campsite. It needs to be "dead out"—no glowing coals, no smoke, no heat. Use water if necessary.

Eating on the Trail

KISS—not the chocolate kind; this stands for "keep it simple and small," a phrase to keep in mind when planning your menu. Meals should be simple to prepare and easy to clean up, and leave you with minimal trash to pack out. For just one night out, you're probably looking at carrying one meal each for breakfast, lunch, and dinner. Each additional night out means you'll add more meals. **Food choices** are many. On the high end you can purchase lightweight, typically expensive, prepackaged freeze-dried meals. On the low end, you might just bring sandwiches or leftovers from home. Choose foods that appeal to you and provide sustained energy.

Dinner should be something you enjoy eating and can look forward to at the end of a day of hiking. It will probably be your most substantial meal.

Breakfast should be quick and easy to prepare, so you can get up, eat, and get going. Make sure it's filling; you don't want to be hungry again when you're only 30 minutes down the trail.

Lunch should require little or no preparation—something you can just pull out and munch. Usually by the time you reach that perfect lunch spot, you're ready to eat.

Snacks are as important as meals. As they say in New Zealand, don't forget your scroggin. Short breaks during the day are good times to reach into a pocket for a handful of trail mix or dried fruit, a nugget of cheese, or maybe even a kiss (the chocolate kind, of course).

Freezer Bag Cooking

Finding food that packs up light and is inexpensive, tasty, easy to prepare, and simple to clean up has always been a challenge for backpackers.

With freezer bag cooking, you assemble all of your meals ahead of time at home, packaging them in individual zip-top freezer bags. To prepare them on the trail, all you do is add boiling water, seal the bag, place it in a homemade insulated pouch called a cozy, and wait about ten minutes. Then eat it right out of the pouch. Cleanup is fast and easy—just wipe off your spoon and tuck the empty bag into your trash.

For those who've struggled for years to find a cost-efficient and easy way to fix appealing meals in the backcountry, this method is a revelation. Learn more in Sarah Svien Kirkconnell's book, *Freezer Bag Cooking*, or visit her website at freezerbagcooking.com, where you can find delicious and inexpensive recipes.

With this simple food system, cozies keep your meal hot.

Safety

Safety on the trail is as much about using good common sense as it is about anything else. Basically it boils down to some basic do's and don't's, plus some things to look out for. Here's a short list.

- Do let someone know your plans for the day before you go.
- Don't hike alone.
- Do dress appropriately and pack the items listed on p. 10.
- Don't start a long hike late in the day.
- Do keep your shoes on while crossing a creek or river.
- Don't cross a waterway in flood.
- Do carry plenty of drinking water.
- Don't drink water straight from the creek.

Natural Hazards

Bears seem to be the number one thing people are afraid of encountering on a backpacking trip. In reality, the chances of meeting a bear on the trail are slim. When you do meet one, the bear usually high-tails it for the nearest laurel thicket. Keep a clean campsite and protect your food at night (see p. 18). Should you meet up with an aggressive bear, stand your ground. These animals can run much faster than you and they can climb trees. Make yourself look and sound as big as possible—wave your arms, shout, bang on something loud. This usually is enough to scare a bear away.

Snakes are the second most feared thing in the woods. Your chances of seeing a snake are good if you spend enough time outside. In the mountains of North and South Carolina there are two types of venomous snakes to be concerned about—copperheads and rattlesnakes (timber, pigmy, and eastern diamondback). Use common sense if you see or hear a snake on the trail. Stop, assess the situation, and wait for the snake to move on or choose an alternate path and go around it.

Stinging Insects—there's nothing worse than bumping into a nest of angry hornets or disturbing a colony of yellow jackets or ground wasps. Such an encounter can quickly turn a peaceful walk in the mountains into a complete panic, with people running pell-mell through the woods screaming and tearing their clothes off. Those stings can hurt like the dickens, and for anyone who is severely allergic they can be deadly. If you have such an allergy, never hike without your epi-pen. And everyone should always be on the lookout; hornets like to build their gray, football-shaped nests over water, so be especially careful around creeks and streams.

Poison ivy, of all the plants in the mountains, seems to be the most prolific, especially in moist woodlands and areas around moving water. You'll want to learn to recognize it. Basically it grows in two ways—as a vine that climbs trees, and as individual plants living in vast colonies on the ground. Wading into a patch or grabbing hold of a hairy vine poses no immediate threat, but wait about 24 hours and if you're allergic (many people are), you'll develop a rash of intensely itchy red blisters wherever the plant touched your skin. If you've had extensive exposure, be prepared to suffer. The rash

The most common venomous snake in the woods is the copperhead.

can take weeks to dry up and go away, often progressing to an oozy mess before it's gone. Should you inadvertently make contact, wash thoroughly with cold water in the nearest stream and hope for the best. If you know you have a strong reaction to poison ivy, there are preparations you can buy over the counter to reduce the effect once you've been exposed. It's worth it to carry some with you.

Crossing Streams

When you approach a stream crossing, size it up. Is it small enough to hop across? Are there stepping-stones, and do they seem stable? How deep is the water? Can you move upstream or downstream to find a better place to cross?

Using trekking poles while crossing a stream adds stability.

If you can hop across or use stepping-stones, by all means do. And if you don't already use a walking stick, look around you for a temporary one. Having three points of contact with the streambed makes you many times more stable. Beware of crossing on logs. Sometimes a log can make for a good bridge, but it can also roll with you or break halfway across. Finally, if the water is more than ankle deep and/or 10 feet or more across, and especially if the bottom looks slippery, unclip the waist strap on your pack (if you fall in you'll want to be able to ditch it in an instant so it won't drag you downstream), clasp your hiking partner(s) by the arms, form a circle, and everyone walk across together. You'll be surprised at how you can negotiate across strong current, over slick rocks, through deep water using this method.

Lightning

Many of the trails in the mountains of North and South Carolina travel along the spines of high ridges. Some are quite exposed with little or no tree cover. These places become especially dangerous in thunderstorms, which are frequent during the hot summer months. You never want to be caught on a high spine in such a storm, but in case you are it's good to know how to minimize the chance of a lightning strike.

If you observe a storm is approaching, get as far off the ridgetop as you can as quickly as possible. Once the storm hits, though, it's time to really take action. That means getting into "lightning position." If you're in a group, spread out, but not so far that you can't make visual and verbal contact. Be careful not to place yourself near the tallest object around, and especially steer clear of rock or cliff overhangs. They may look safe and dry, but the potential for "ground lightning" here is high. Get in the habit of carrying a small closed-cell foam pad in an accessible spot on the outside of your pack. This could be your sleeping pad, a camp chair (see pp. 13 & 21), or just a small piece of foam for this exact purpose. Remove your pack, take the pad out, and get on it immediately. You can squat or sit. You want to reduce the amount of direct contact with the ground as much as you comfortably can. Be prepared to stay put for however long it takes the storm to pass.

Waterfalls

Every year people die at waterfalls, and some have died at waterfalls listed in this book. Here's what usually happens. They try to climb up the cliff or steep slope beside a waterfall to get a better view or take a picture or make an attempt to reach the top, and then they slip and fall. They try to peer over the edge at the top, and then they slip and fall. They try to climb the waterfall itself, and then they slip and fall. Everything near a waterfall— rocks, roots, fallen trees—is wet and slippery. If you do any of these things, it's only a matter of time before you slip and fall, too. At best you'll twist an ankle or break an arm; at worst it could be fatal. Certainly your mistake will ruin what could have been a nice hike for you and everyone else. *Always exercise extreme caution and common sense around waterfalls.*

Waterfalls are beautiful, but they can also be dangerous.

Hunting Season

During the fall and on select spring dates, if you're hiking in the national forest there's a chance you'll run into game hunters. Most of the time, especially during small game season, this is not a problem. However, on opening day of rifle deer hunting season, around major holidays, and during bear season it *can* be a big deal. On these days, in some places, it can seem that the woods are full of hunters—and you might not be comfortable with that. Regardless, it's a good idea to wear bright colors in the woods during hunting seasons. For specific hunting dates in North Carolina check the website at ncwildlife.org, or for South Carolina at dnr.sc.gov. Hunting is not allowed at any time in South Carolina state parks or Great Smoky Mountains National Park, so they are a safe bet all year long.

Injuries and Emergencies in the Backcountry

Blisters are by far the most common (and annoying) injury on a backpacking overnight trip. Avoiding them is easy—just make sure you have footwear that fits properly, and pay attention. While hiking, check in on your feet regularly. Notice a hot spot? Deal with it immediately. That could mean something as simple as adjusting your socks—or as time-consuming as stopping to apply moleskin. If you let the hot spot bloom into a blister, you'll be pretty uncomfortable for the duration of the trip. **Prevention** is the key to avoiding injuries in the backcountry. Use your head and don't take unnecessary risks. Still, injuries can and will occur. With your first aid kit (see p. 18), you'll be able to handle most minor problems.
Getting help may become necessary should catastrophe strike, but before you request assistance, realize what you are doing. Calling or signalling for outside help in a backcountry situation is a very, very big deal. Your plea for help will set off a long sequence of events. Volunteer rescuers from across the region will drop whatever they are doing to rush to your aid. Professional services that may include park rangers, ambulance drivers, and even helicopter pilots will kick into gear. Media crews will send in their people, hoping to make the evening news. It's costly in both time and money. There is a good chance you'll be charged a fee for any professional services, and that charge will be justifiably high.

You want to be absolutely certain your situation warrants this type of response. If it does, you have limited choices for how to get help.
Few places in the backcountry receive a cell phone signal, although you might get lucky from a high ridge. Don't count on it, but it's always worth a try.

Another tool on the market these days is a personal locator device (PLD), which uses GPS technology to send out locator signals and can also be used to signal for aid. Most likely, though, your only means of getting help will be for one of your party to go out and look for it. Before sending someone for assistance, always make sure the person you're sending knows the exact location and extent of injuries to the victim.

Great Smoky Mountains National Park

Contact Information

Great Smoky Mountains
National Park
107 Park Headquarters Rd
Gatlinburg, TN 37738
865-436-1200
www.nps.gov/grsm

Backcountry Reservations
www.smokiespermits.nps.gov
865-436-1297

Permit Required	Yes
Fee	$4 pp pn
Max Group Size	8
Pets Allowed	No

pp=per person pn=per night

Great Smoky Mountains National Park is the premier backpacking destination in the southeastern United States, boasting over 800 miles of trails, 98 backcountry campsites, and 15 trail shelters. Hikers can expect well-maintained trails marked with easy-to-follow signs. Seventy-one miles of the Appalachian National Scenic Trail traverse the Park, following the high ridges that mark the state line between North Carolina and Tennessee. All campsites are located near a water source and have cable systems for hanging food, and all shelters have privies. For the most part, trailheads are located on easy-to-navigate paved roads with ample parking. You're allowed to stay up to three consecutive nights in the same campsite, one night only in a shelter.

In 2013, GSMNP instituted a use fee for backcountry shelters and campsites in the park. The fee is $4 per night with a $20 maximum per person. Reservations can be made 24 hours a day, 7 days a week at the GSMNP backcountry reservations website, where you can also find information on site availability and the number of people reserved for a particular date. Alternatively, reservations can be made in person at the park headquarters backcountry office in Gatlinburg.

Mount Cammerer

Difficulty	Moderate
Hike Distance	17.3 miles
Type of Hike	Loop
Total Ascent	4,210 ft
Land Manager	NPS
Fee	$4 pp pn

pp=per person pn=per night

The historic Mt. Cammerer Lookout offers a fantastic view.

The far eastern section of the Great Smokies where Big Creek comes crashing into the Pigeon River sees fewer visitors than any other area, even though it is close to I-40. Maybe that's because driving the highway through the Pigeon River Gorge can be intimidating. Be brave and give it a go—you'll be glad you did.

On this long but not too difficult circuit you'll spend your first day hiking along beautiful Big Creek. On the second day you'll climb up to traverse the high ridgeline that separates North Carolina from Tennessee. What a contrast! Big Creek Trail is wide and ascends very slowly as it passes through a dense canopy of trees and rhododendron past several waterfalls. Rest up for day two, which begins with a long climb up to the Appalachian Trail. The views open up as you work your way up to Mt. Cammerer Lookout. The lookout is the highlight of the trip and a great place to stop for a break, eat lunch, and take in the view before the long downhill back to Big Creek.

Getting to the Trailhead

From exit 4 on I-40 just inside Tennessee, follow Waterville Road past the powerhouse on the Pigeon River, across Mt. Sterling Road, and finally to the farthest trailhead parking area at Big Creek Campground, a total of 3.4 miles.

GPS Coordinates

N 35° 45.09′ W 83° 06.58′

Hiking Directions

Begin Walk around the gate and up Big Creek Trail. It's an old road at this point, and you'll follow Big Creek all the way to your campsite.

Mile 1.5 Pass Midnight Hole Falls on the left. This is an excellent swimming hole in warm weather.

Mile 2.1 Pass Mouse Creek Falls on the left, a 40-foot drop from a side creek that falls into Big Creek.

Mile 5.5 Cross the bridge and enter campsite #37, your only camping option on this entire loop. It's a large site with numerous spots all along the creek. The wooded glade makes for a peaceful setting, and after periods of wet weather, there is a nice little waterfall right near one of the tent areas. Drinking and cooking water is plentiful from Big Creek.

Mile 5.5 Just beyond the campsite, turn right on Low Gap Trail, which quickly takes you up and away from Big Creek.

Mile 8.1 A steady 3-mile climb brings you to the Appalachian Trail. Turn right to follow the ridgeline and the state line.

Mile 10.2 Turn left on Mt. Cammerer Trail, leading to the lookout.

Mile 10.8 Reach Mt. Cammerer Lookout. Enjoy the views from this impressive structure, which clings to the edge of White Rock. When you're ready, return to the AT.

After heavy rains, Mouse Creek Falls is a dramatic sight.

Mount Cammerer (cont.)

Mile 11.4 Turn left, back onto the AT.

Mile 13.6 Lower Mt. Cammerer Trail exits left. Stay on the AT.

Mile 14.5 Turn right on Chestnut Branch Trail.

Mile 15.6 The trail ends at the road through Big Creek Campground. Turn right to walk the road back to the trailhead.

Mile 17.3 Finish.

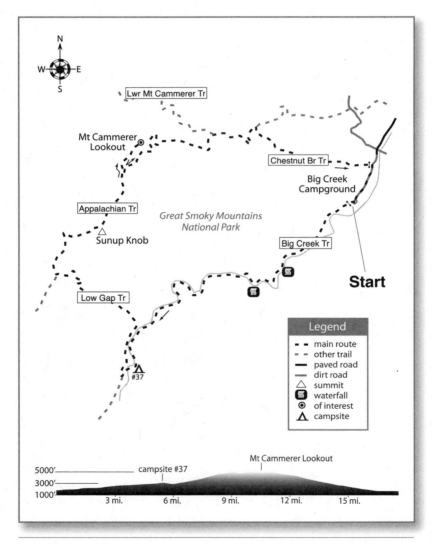

Hemphill Bald

Hemphill Bald Trail follows right along the park boundary with Cataloochee Ranch.

Difficulty	Moderate
Hike Distance	13.9 miles
Type of Hike	Loop
Total Ascent	2,940 ft
Land Manager	NPS
Fee	$4 pp pn

pp=per person pn=per night

*B*ecause this route starts at Polls Gap, you can hike it only during the late spring, summer, or fall. The main reason is that the road to the trailhead is closed over the winter months. But even if you accessed this loop from a lower trailhead, given the higher elevations you'd be more likely to encounter deep snow on the trail in winter, which makes the other three seasons better times to go in any case.

On the first day you'll get to experience a full day of backpacking downhill. It's not too steep, which is easier on the knees. It's a great way to begin a trip, but prepare yourself for payback time—an uphill start on the second day. Pay attention to the woods around you as you leave Polls Gap. Notice how the yellow birch trees disappear as you leave the higher elevations, and by the time you reach Caldwell Fork you're in a stand of tulip poplar.

Day two has you climbing for the first half as you make your way to the top of Hemphill Bald, where the view is pretty awesome. Once up high, you stay high all the way to the end.

Hemphill Bald (cont.)

Getting to the Trailhead

Take the Blue Ridge Parkway north from Cherokee or south from Soco Gap near Maggie Valley to Heintooga Ridge Road (near milepost 458). Once on Heintooga Ridge Road, travel 6.2 miles to the Polls Gap trailhead.

Note: Heintooga Road is closed from November 1 to May 11.

GPS Coordinates

N 35° 33.79' W 83° 09.70'

Hiking Directions

Begin Walk down Rough Fork Trail. Looking at the woods from the parking lot, this is the trail on the left. Enjoy the first 5 miles; it's mostly all downhill.

Mile 3.5 Turn right on Caldwell Fork Trail.

Mile 4.8 Reach an area known as Big Poplars. Once you see the trees, you'll know how it got its name.

Mile 5.1 Here you'll enter campsite #41, next to Caldwell Fork. This pretty site has ample room. Several groups could spread out to the different flat spots and still have plenty of privacy. This site is frequently used by horsepackers, so you can expect to either see horses or what they typically leave behind. Your water source is Caldwell Fork, at this point still a bold stream.

Mile 5.3 After your night out, continue across Caldwell Fork and turn right on Hemphill Bald Trail.

Mile 8.4 A 3-mile steady but not steep climb brings you to Double Gap and a fenceline with a large pasture on the other side. Turn right here without crossing through the fence stile to continue on Hemphill Bald Trail. The Cataloochee Divide Trail goes off to the left here.

Mile 9.2 Reach the summit of Hemphill Bald. This is a good spot to take a break after your long climb. You'll find a stone table ideal for eating lunch and enjoying the view. From here you've got close to 5 miles to go to the trailhead. It's high altitude hiking at its best with wildflowers galore and the occasional view through the trees.

Mile 13.9 Finish.

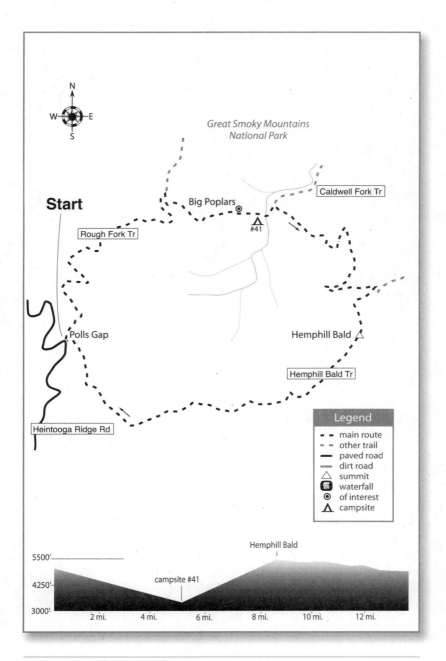

Start

Great Smoky Mountains
National Park

Big Poplars

Caldwell Fork Tr

#41

Rough Fork Tr

Hemphill Bald

Polls Gap

Hemphill Bald Tr

Heintooga Ridge Rd

Legend

- - - main route
- - - other trail
— paved road
— dirt road
△ summit
♨ waterfall
◉ of interest
▲ campsite

Hemphill Bald

5500'

campsite #41

4250'

3000'

2 mi.　4 mi.　6 mi.　8 mi.　10 mi.　12 mi.

Icewater Spring

Difficulty	Moderate
Hike Distance	15 miles
Type of Hike	Loop
Total Ascent	3,877 ft
Land Manager	NPS
Fee	$4 pp pn

pp=per person pn=per night

Icewater Spring Shelter sits high in the cloud forest at close to 6,000 feet.

When you're walking along the high spine of the Smokies as you do on the Appalachian Trail, finding a reliable water source is not always easy. Creeks and streams are commonplace lower down, but up here it's almost always a spring you'll be looking for. A good spring is reason enough for a shelter location, and the one at Icewater Spring Shelter lives up to its name—it's cold as ice.

On this hike you have the option of spending two nights out, each one at a different shelter. Just a couple of miles from the trailhead, you'll reach Kephart Shelter, named for Horace Kephart, a writer and one of the driving forces behind the creation of Great Smoky Mountains National Park. A big climb follows, the highlight of which is the spectacular clifftop view from Charlies Bunion. Horace Kephart named this crag after his mountain guide Charlie Conner. Mr. Kephart had quite a sense of humor, sometimes at others' expense. Your home for the night at Icewater Spring is a "room with a view," a classic Smokies trail shelter, open in front with a world of mountain ridges below.

Getting to the Trailhead

From Oconaluftee Visitor Center north of Cherokee, travel 7.0 miles on US 441. The route begins at Kephart Prong Trailhead on the east side of the highway.

GPS Coordinates
N 35° 35.15' W 83° 21.50'

Hiking Directions

Begin Walk across the footbridge and up Kephart Prong Trail.

Mile 2.1 Reach Kephart Shelter, a two-level, open-front building with platform sleeping for 14. To turn this into a two-night excursion, you can stay here on either the first or the second night. Water is available from nearby Kephart Prong. To begin the loop, turn right on Grassy Branch Trail.

Mile 5.0 A long, steady climb brings you to Dry Sluice Gap Trail. Turn left.

Mile 6.2 Turn left here on the Appalachian Trail. You'll now be walking the spine of the Smokies, which marks the state line between North Carolina and Tennessee. Great views abound.

Mile 6.7 A right turn here takes you out a short trail to Charlies Bunion, a heavily visited clifftop view. After this short side trip, continue on along the AT.

Mile 7.7 Look for the pipe spring here on the right. This is the best water source for Icewater Spring Shelter, just ahead.

Mile 7.8 Reach Icewater Spring Shelter. The platform sleeping arrangement will accommodate 14 people. Water is available at the spring located at mile 7.7. It's a great place to spend the night. In the morning, continue southbound on the AT.

Mile 8.2 Boulevard Trail exits. Continue on the AT.

Mile 9.2 Turn left to begin a delightfully long downhill on Sweat Heifer Creek Trail.

Charlies Bunion looks north across the Tennessee Valley.

Icewater Spring (cont.)

Mile 11.1 Cross a section of Sweat Heifer Creek Falls.

Mile 12.9 Return to Kephart Shelter and close the hiking loop.

Continue back onto Kephart Prong Trail.

Mile 15.0 Finish.

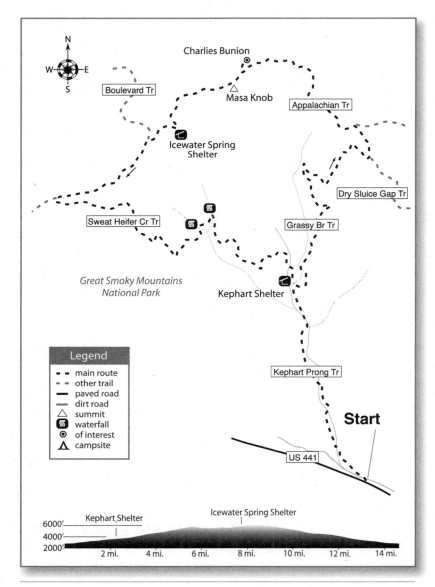

Poke Patch

Difficulty	Moderate
Hike Distance	8.2 miles
Type of Hike	Out & Back
Total Ascent	1,741 ft
Land Manager	NPS
Fee	$4 pp pn

pp=per person pn=per night

Each campsite in the Smokies is marked with a signpost.

Deep Creek Trail has the distinction of being one of the very first officially designated trails in the Great Smoky Mountains National Park. From its high-altitude start near Newfound Gap to its end near Bryson City, it travels just over 14 miles. Some folks like to set a shuttle and take several days and nights to hike the whole thing, stopping at pristine spots along the way to trout fish or just hang out by the creek.

This overnight trip takes you to the uppermost campsite on Deep Creek, a spot known as Poke Patch. It makes for a fine night's outing. If you get an early start, not only will you have time to enjoy an afternoon of noodling by the creek, you will also likely have your pick of the best camping spot. Be sure to check out both sides of the creek.

If trout fishing is your thing, there is plenty of water to choose from. Fish this far upstream are as wild as they come. And yes, as you can see from the elevation profile, it's a downhill walk to get there. Not to worry, with a good night's rest and a healthy dose of mountain air, your climb out the next morning should be a breeze.

Poke Patch (cont.)

Getting to the Trailhead

From the Oconaluftee Visitor Center north of Cherokee, travel 14.0 miles on US 441. The route begins at the Deep Creek Trailhead on the west side of the highway.

GPS Coordinates

N 35° 35.89' W 83° 25.27'

Hiking Directions

Begin From the parking lot, walk about 500 feet up the road (north) to where Deep Creek Trail exits downhill into the woods. There is a small pullout beside the road here. Once on the trail, you'll begin to drop into the Deep Creek watershed. It's a steady descent all the way to your destination.

Mile 2.1 Reach an area where the creek bed and the trail are one. Depending on how much recent rain there has been, it may require some hopping from one side of the streambed to the other.

Mile 2.8 Down on the right next to the creek, you can see where folks have made a camping spot. This is not an official campsite. Continue down the trail.

Mile 4.1 Reach campsite #53, right on the shore of Deep Creek. This spot is called Poke Patch and at one time must have been a spot where mountain folk collected poke weed, a spring delicacy. This small site has room for 4 to 5 tents, and getting water from Deep Creek is easy. After your night out, return up the trail the way you came down.

Mile 8.2 Finish.

Dog hobble grows in thick tangles in the low places alongside Deep Creek.

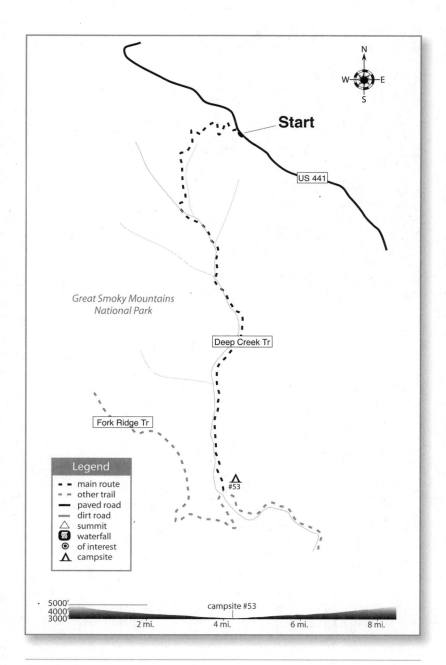

Start

US 441

Great Smoky Mountains
National Park

Deep Creek Tr

Fork Ridge Tr

⛺
#53

Legend
- - - main route
- - - other trail
— paved road
— dirt road
△ summit
♨ waterfall
⊙ of interest
⛺ campsite

N
W ⊛ E
S

5000'
4000'
3000'
      2 mi.   4 mi.   6 mi.   8 mi.
              campsite #53

Forney Creek

Difficulty	Strenuous
Hike Distance	20.3 miles
Type of Hike	Loop
Total Ascent	5,010 ft
Land Manager	NPS
Fee	$4 pp pn

pp=per person pn=per night

You'll ford Forney Creek seven times before you're done.

On day one of this excursion you'll spend most of the time walking downhill, dropping 4,000 feet in ten miles. That's quite a descent! Leaving the spruce-fir forest of the high Smokies, you'll cross Andrews Bald with its wild azaleas and tromp down into the lush valley formed by Forney Creek. Take your time, use some trekking poles, and be careful to not wear out your knees. A choice of campsites awaits, all right on the banks of Forney Creek. If you've got the legs to make it all the way to campsite #68 in one day or you decide to make it a two-night trip, you'll find #68 to be one of the choicest in the Park. It's not often you can sleep within spitting distance of a such a lovely waterfall.

Day two is the day you pay for all that luxurious downhill hiking. Yes, you must now regain the elevation you lost on day one. It's not as bad as it might seem, though; Forney Creek Trail follows the route of an old narrow-gauge logging railway. You'll see remnants of it in an old wall and several trestle crossings. Watch the weather—the fords on Forney Creek can become treacherous in high water.

Getting to the Trailhead

From Oconaluftee Visitor Center north of Cherokee, drive US 441 to the state line at Newfound Gap. Turn left on Clingmans Dome Road and continue 7.0 miles to the large trailhead parking lot at the end of the road.

Note: Clingmans Dome Road is closed from December 1 to March 15.

GPS Coordinates
N 35° 33.39′ W 83° 29.76′

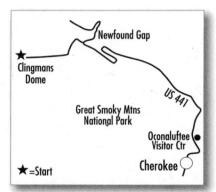

Hiking Directions

Begin From the far end of the parking area, walk around the information board and onto the Appalachian Trail Bypass/Connector Trail.

Mile 0.2 Turn left onto Forney Ridge Trail and head down into the spruce fir forest.

Mile 1.1 Forney Creek Trail enters from the right. This is where you'll come back up at the end of your trip. Continue straight on.

Mile 1.7 Reach Andrews Bald, where you can take a break and enjoy the view. Once you leave the bald, the trail changes character, becoming wet, rocky, and much less used.

Mile 5.5 Turn right on Springhouse Branch Trail.

Mile 9.8 Finally you'll bottom out here as you reach campsite #71, which is 4,000 feet lower than where you started! This is a very large and quite pretty campsite located at an old homesite; you can't miss the old chimney. Get your water from nearby Forney Creek or the spring you passed just before the campsite. There are three more sites to choose from farther up the creek, but if you're ready to call it a day, this is it for you. To continue the route, turn right here on Forney Creek Trail.

Mile 11.4 Jonas Creek Trail exits to the left here. Also, campsite #70 is just across the bridge. This is a large campsite with room for lots of tents. The creek provides your water. Continue to follow Forney Creek, which you will ford multiple times.

Mile 13.0 Reach campsite #69, a medium-sized site with room for at least six tents. The creek provides your water.

Mile 16.7 Reach lower campsite #68. This small site has room for just a few tents and really is not all that nice. Drinking water is from the adjacent stream.

Mile 17.2 Reach upper campsite #68, which is right next to a

Forney Creek (cont.)

lovely waterfall. It's one of the most idyllic camping spots in the entire park. This, too, is a small site with room for just a tent or so. It would be perfect for a hammock camper.

Mile 19.2 After climbing for what seems forever, turn left, back onto Forney Ridge Trail.

Mile 20.1 Turn right on the AT Bypass Trail.

Mile 20.3 Finish.

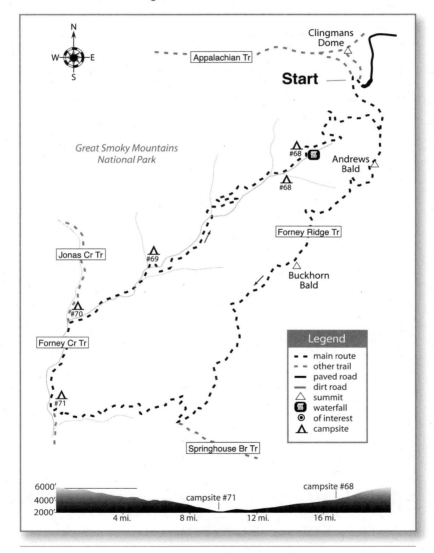

The Narrows

The shelter on the Appalachian Trail at Doublespring Gap is great for a break.

Difficulty	Strenuous
Hike Distance	19.4 miles
Type of Hike	Loop
Total Ascent	4,750 ft
Land Manager	NPS
Fee	$4 pp pn

pp=per person pn=per night

High-altitude trailheads have their perks: Start at daybreak and you're likely to be treated to a stunning sunrise, and chances are, much of your first day's hike will be downhill. Such is the case with this route, which begins just below Clingmans Dome, the second highest point in the East. Your first day takes you along Forney Creek, where you'll find three campsites to choose from. The first is beside a waterfall—a good alternative should you start late in the day or plan to be out more than one night. Your best bet for the night is campsite #70, where Jonas Creek enters Forney Creek. It's about halfway along the route at the point where you'll begin your uphill portion of the expedition. Be aware that you'll spend a lot of time crossing and recrossing both Forney and Jonas Creeks. You will undoubtedly get your feet wet and should be cautious if either is running in flood.

The highlight of this hike occurs on day two. Once you reach the Appalachian Trail, you'll walk the backbone of the Smokies on a section known as The Narrows. It's a top-of-the-world-feeling kind of place.

The Narrows (cont.)

Getting to the Trailhead

From Oconaluftee Visitor Center north of Cherokee, follow US 441 to the state line at Newfound Gap. Turn left on Clingmans Dome Road and go 7.0 miles to the large trailhead parking lot at its end.
Note: Clingmans Dome Road is closed from December 1 to March 15.

GPS Coordinates

N 35° 33.39' W 83° 29.76'

Hiking Directions

Begin From the far end of the parking area, walk around the information board and onto the Appalachian Trail Bypass/Connector Trail.

Mile 0.2 Turn left on Forney Ridge Trail.

Mile 1.1 Turn right on Forney Creek Trail.

Mile 3.0 Reach upper campsite #68. This small but beautiful spot is at the base of a pretty waterfall. If you're starting late or making this into a two-night outing, make your camp here. Water is easily obtainable from the adjacent creek.

Mile 3.5 Reach lower campsite #68, also small, but not so nice. Get water from the creek.

Mile 7.0 After several stream fords, reach campsite #69. This pretty site has room for a good number of tents on several levels. Water is from the creek. There are stream fords downstream.

Mile 8.4 Turn right across the footbridge on Jonas Creek Trail. Immediately on the right is campsite #70, a large site with lots of room to spread out. Drinking and cooking water are from the creek. This is the last campsite before you reach Double Spring Gap Shelter, 8 miles away. Even more stream fords are up ahead.

Mile 12.6 Turn right on Welch Ridge Trail.

Mile 13.3 Hazel Creek Trail exits here on the left. Continue on Welch Ridge Trail.

Mile 15.0 Turn right on the AT. The next mile or so of trail crosses The Narrows, a section that follows a high, knifelike ridge. With open views in all directions, it's an exhilarating and energizing place to walk.

Mile 16.3 Reach Double Spring Gap Shelter, a two-tier structure that sleeps 12 on platforms. Water is available from a nearby spring. It would take a strong hiker to make it here in one day, but if you're out for two nights, this is an ideal spot for the second night. Otherwise, it's a great spot to take a break.

Mile 16.8 Goshen Prong Trail exits left here; stay on the AT.

More stunning views will follow.

Mile 18.7 Turn right on Bypass Trail and follow it to the finish.

Mile 19.4 Finish.

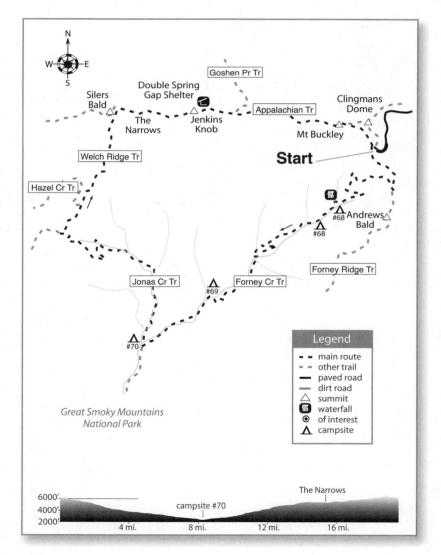

Great Smoky Mountains National Park

Deep Creek

Difficulty	Easier
Hike Distance	5.4 miles
Type of Hike	Out & Back
Total Ascent	800 ft
Land Manager	NPS
Fee	$4 pp pn

pp=per person   pn=per night

You'll pass Tom Branch Falls shortly after beginning your hike.

An overnight trip to Deep Creek is a must-do for anyone camping in the backcountry of the Great Smokies. It's easy to get to—right outside the town of Bryson City—and great any time of the year. Always a favorite with the wildflower crowd, the woods are full of blooms from early spring through the fall. In the summertime near the trailhead you'll pass families carrying tubes to float the creek, a great way to cool off on a hot day. Autumn leaves add exciting color as they swirl down the stream and make a great backdrop for the waterfalls along the route. And of course winter brings solitude—you're likely to have the creek to yourself.

Many folks choose the hike to campsite #60 for an introductory overnight backpacking trip. If you've got youngsters along, the distance is just about right and the trail is not technically difficult, with much of it following an old road. With the creek always nearby, there's plenty to see along the way.

Getting to the Trailhead

Follow the brown GSMNP Deep Creek signs from downtown Bryson City out West Deep Creek Road and into the park. The trailhead parking lot is beyond the picnic area.

GPS Coordinates
N 35° 27.85' W 83° 26.05'

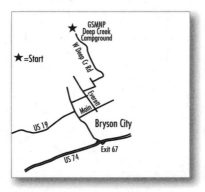

Hiking Directions

Begin Walk past the gate at the turnout and up Deep Creek Trail, which at this point is an old road.

Mile 0.8 Continue straight on as Indian Creek Trail enters from the right.

Mile 0.9 After crossing two bridges, you'll see the Horse Bypass Trail entering from the left. You may encounter horses from here on.

Mile 1.9 Just after crossing a bridge, Loop Trail enters on the right. If you want to see something different on your return trip,

you can take this trail up and over Sunkota Ridge, turn right on Indian Creek Trail, and return to Deep Creek that way. For now, bear left upstream to remain on Deep Creek Trail.

Mile 2.2 The trail leaves the creek here at a turnaround and heads to the right, up the side of the gorge.

Mile 2.7 Reach campsite #60, your home for the evening. This site is named Bumgardner Branch for the small stream you cross just before you arrive there. You'll find space for numerous tents and room to spread out somewhat if there are folks already set up to camp. Water is plentiful; Deep Creek flows right past the campsite. From here you'll return the way you came.

Mile 5.4 Finish.

Don't be surprised if you see a horse or two on this hike.

Deep Creek Map

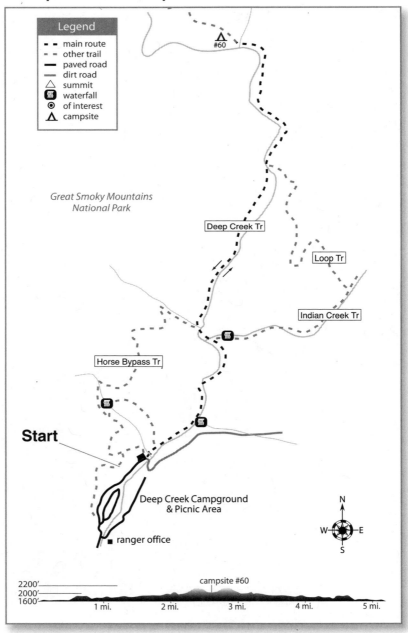

Legend
- - - main route
- - - other trail
— paved road
— dirt road
△ summit
▥ waterfall
◉ of interest
▲ campsite

△ #60

Great Smoky Mountains National Park

Deep Creek Tr

Loop Tr

Indian Creek Tr

Horse Bypass Tr

Start

Deep Creek Campground & Picnic Area

■ ranger office

N
W—＋—E
S

campsite #60

2200'
2000'
1600'
1 mi.   2 mi.   3 mi.   4 mi.   5 mi.

Bryson Place

Difficulty	Moderate
Hike Distance	13.7 miles
Type of Hike	Loop
Total Ascent	2,300 ft
Land Manager	NPS
Fee	$4 pp pn

pp=per person pn=per night

Indian Creek Falls is a favorite destination for waterfall photographers who don't want to walk too far.

Overnight backpacking on the lower stretches of Deep and Indian Creeks opens up a lot of options. It's one of the few trail loops on the North Carolina side of the park that has more than just one or two campsites to choose from. On this loop, you have your choice of five different spots. You may even want to extend the trip and spend an additional night. High priority, though, is to spend a night on the banks of Deep Creek. This idyllic stream rushes down from the high reaches of the park, alternately crashing against boulders and resting in quiet pools as it follows its course. While hiking, it's not uncommon to see majestic kingfishers dart and swoop above the stream, pursuing food and protecting their territory. Nor will wildflower enthusiasts be disappointed. Early spring through fall, the forest floor displays everything from trillium to cardinal flower. And if you like to fish, the creeks are full of trout. What's the best site to choose? It's hard to go wrong with any of them.

Bryson Place (cont.)

Getting to the Trailhead

Follow the brown GSMNP Deep Creek signs from downtown Bryson City out West Deep Creek Road and into the park. The trailhead parking lot is beyond the picnic area.

GPS Coordinates

N 35° 27.85' W 83° 26.05'

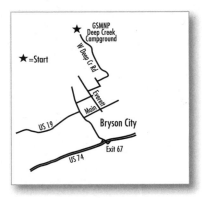

Hiking Directions

Begin Walk past the gate at the turnout and up the Deep Creek Trail, which at this point is an old road.

Mile 0.8 Turn right on Indian Creek Trail. Soon you'll pass Indian Creek Falls on the left.

Mile 1.3 Stone Pile Gap Trail exits on the right.

Mile 1.6 Loop Trail exits on the left.

Mile 3.8 Deep Low Gap Trail exits on the right.

Mile 4.5 Reach campsite #46. This small, little-used campsite is a good place to spend the night if you want to stay out more than one night on this loop—especially if getting a late start. Water is available from a small nearby stream.

Mile 6.0 Cross Sunkota Ridge Trail and begin downhill.

Mile 7.5 Reach campsite #57. Known as Bryson Place, this spot was a favorite campsite of Horace Kephart, one of the founders of the Great Smoky Mountains National Park. Located right on Deep Creek, it is large and very popular with the horse crowd.

Mile 8.1 Reach campsite #58, a much smaller but very nice site that does not allow horses. Again, water is available from Deep Creek.

Mile 8.9 Reach campsite #59, another very nice smaller site right on Deep Creek.

Mile 11.0 Reach campsite #60. This is the last site you'll pass on Deep Creep. Like #57, it allows horse users.

Mile 11.8 Loop Trail enters from the left.

Mile 12.8 The Horse Bypass Trail exits on the right.

Mile 12.9 You'll close the loop as you reach Indian Creek Trail.

Mile 13.7 Finish.

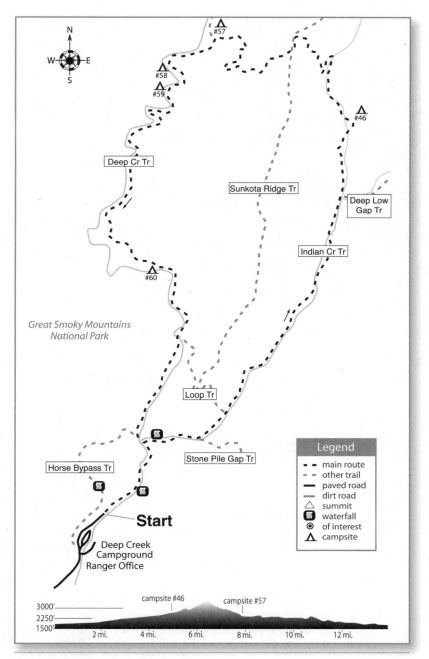

Great Smoky Mountains National Park

Goldmine Loop

Difficulty	Easier
Hike Distance	3.8 miles
Type of Hike	Loop
Total Ascent	765 ft
Land Manager	NPS
Fee	$4 pp pn

pp=per person pn=per night

Good signage helps you find your way in Great Smoky Mountains National Park.

Chances are you won't find any gold on this overnight. But you will find a fantastic short hike with plenty of interesting things to see, and a surprisingly little-used campsite to spend the night.

On the drive to the trailhead, don't be too concerned when you see the sign near the park entrance that reads "Welcome to a Road to Nowhere…." Folks around these parts are still miffed about a broken promise to build a road along the north shore of Lake Fontana all the way to Fontana Dam. Road crews got as far as building a tunnel years ago before the project was abandoned. A few people still believe it might yet be completed. What we're left with is a nice road out to a tunnel, where the road ends. The great thing is that there's a lot to see and do in this "nowhere." You'll rediscover old homesites, have a chance for a swim in the lake if it's warm, and hike along a relatively short and easy track to a beautiful campsite. To top it off, you get to hike back through the 1,200-foot dark tunnel at the end of the trip.

Getting to the Trailhead

From downtown Bryson City, go north out of town on Fontana Road. When you reach the park boundary, the road becomes Lakeview Drive. It's 9.0 miles to the trailhead, which is located at the last parking area before the tunnel.

GPS Coordinates
N 35° 27.53' W 83° 32.27'

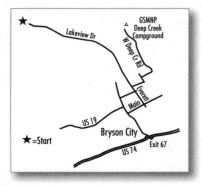

Hiking Directions

Begin Walk across the road and onto Goldmine Loop Trail.

Mile 0.5 Tunnel Bypass Trail exits to the right along the ridge. Bear left to stay on Goldmine Loop.

Mile 1.3 After following a creek you'll reach the shore of Lake Fontana. If the water is low, you can see the remnants of an old stone wall leading out into the lake bed. In summer, this is a good spot to take a swim.

Mile 1.7 Turn right off Goldmine Loop Trail onto the access trail leading to campsite #67.

Mile 1.9 Reach campsite #67. This is where you'll spend the night. If you look closely you'll see this area was once the field of an old homestead. Old homesites like this make for great campsites. There's plenty of level ground and space for 3 to 4 tents. Water is from a small stream adjacent to the site. After your night out, return to Goldmine Loop.

Mile 2.1 Continue back onto Goldmine Loop Trail.

Mile 2.7 Pass through an old homestead. Look for the chimney.

Mile 3.0 A short but steep climb brings you up to a right turn onto Lakeshore Trail.

Mile 3.1 Tunnel Bypass Trail exits right. Stay straight.

Mile 3.2 Reach the tunnel. You may want to wear your headlamp for this.

Mile 3.8 Finish.

The walk through the tunnel is an interesting way to end your hike.

Goldmine Loop Map

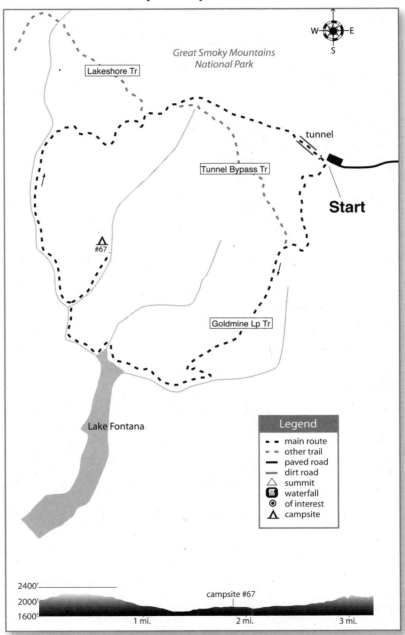

Great Smoky Mountains
National Park

Lakeshore Tr

tunnel

Tunnel Bypass Tr

Start

△ #67

Goldmine Lp Tr

Lake Fontana

Legend

- - main route
- - other trail
— paved road
— dirt road
△ summit
▦ waterfall
◉ of interest
▲ campsite

2400'
2000'
1600'

campsite #67

1 mi.   2 mi.   3 mi.

Shuckstack Tower

Difficulty	Moderate
Hike Distance	12 miles
Type of Hike	Loop
Total Ascent	3,373 ft
Land Manager	NPS
Fee	$4 pp pn

pp=per person pn=per night

Climbing to the top of Shuckstack Tower is an experience you won't soon forget.

Looking for a great view and a little derring-do? You'll find both on this hike to the Shuckstack Lookout Tower. For years the forests of our country were monitored for fires from tall towers, many atop lonely outcrops of rock. Most towers have disappeared as more modern approaches to fire control have taken over, but a small number still stand in our southern Appalachian mountains. You can still climb the steep steps and enter the glass-enclosed box that gently sways with the wind atop the Shuckstack Tower. For some it's a white-knuckle experience, but if you're there for the view, it's well worth it.

This loop hike will take you high above the shores of Lake Fontana to campsite #91, known as Upper Lost Cove, which is situated on a delightful stream—a stream you'll become quite familiar with as you cross and recross it more than a dozen times. On day two you're in for a climb right off the bat as you'll ascend steeply to the Appalachian Trail and finally to the tower. Enjoy the view!

Getting to the Trailhead

From Robbinsville, take NC 143 east for 9.0 miles. Turn left on NC 28 and go 10.3 miles to the Fontana Dam entrance road. Turn right and drive 2.4 miles out and across the top of the dam to the end of the road.

GPS Coordinates

N 35° 27.63' W 83° 48.65'

Hiking Directions

Begin From the parking lot, walk out Lakeshore Trail, a mix of singletrack and old road. This section remains well above the lake.

Mile 5.2 Turn left on Lost Cove Trail (turning right would take you to campsite #90, about a mile off the route) and begin following the creek upstream, where there are several places to cross. You should be able to rockhop across, but during wet weather, expect to get your feet wet.

Mile 6.0 Reach campsite #91, your best option for a night out on this loop. This small site has room for about 4 tents. Water is easily obtained from Lost Cove Creek, which rushes right by. Get a good night's sleep, as you'll need your rest for the next morning. From here up to the Appalachian Trail, the trail climbs steeply.

Mile 8.0 Breath easy now, you're at the top. Turn left here on the AT.

Mile 8.4 At a hairpin turn in the trail atop the spine, turn left on an unmarked but frequently used trail. This leads to Shuckstack Tower.

Mile 8.5 Reach the tower, which sits atop a rocky outcrop. Climb on up for a breathtaking view. This is a great spot to take a break before returning to the trailhead. When you've had enough, head back to the AT and continue the long walk down the mountain.

Mile 12.0 Finish.

You can see Fontana Lake from the top of Shuckstack Tower.

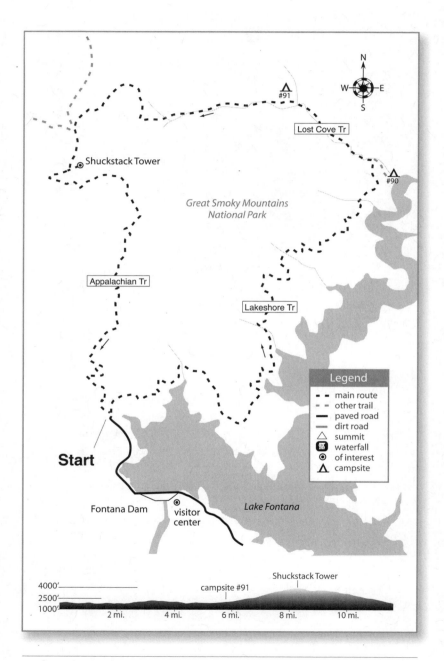

Twentymile

Difficulty	Easier
Hike Distance	5.2 miles
Type of Hike	Out & Back
Total Ascent	800 ft
Land Manager	NPS
Fee	$4 pp pn

pp=per person pn=per night

Crossing a classic Smokies log footbridge over a waterfall is an act of bravery.

Don't worry, this route is not 20 miles long! The name comes from Twentymile Creek, located 20 miles from the confluence of the Little Tennessee and Tuckaseegee rivers. In case you're wondering, there is no Tenmile Creek or Sevenmile Creek, so why there is a Twentymile Creek is anyone's guess. Regardless, this backpacking overnight begins and ends at Twentymile Ranger Station and follows first Twentymile Creek and then Dalton Branch, ending in one of the most delightful campsites in the Great Smoky Mountains National Park.

Whether it's your first-ever overnight or you are a seasoned backpacker, you'll enjoy this hike. Like many trails in the park, this one follows a rushing stream for its entirety. You'll get plenty of practice crossing the park's standard one-log bridges; there are quite a few along the route. The first crosses over the top of a small waterfall. Helpful hint: Take the bridges one person at a time and use the hand rail only for balance, not to lean against.

Getting to the Trailhead

From the bridge on NC 28 that crosses Lake Cheoah just below Fontana Dam, drive 5.4 miles to the Twentymile Ranger Station. Trailhead parking is just beyond the office.

GPS Coordinates
N 35° 28.04' W 83° 52.60'

provides plenty of water for cooking and filling your bottles. After a good sleep, return to Twentymile the same way you hiked in—or if you're game for an additional 3.7 miles and another 300 feet of elevation gain, circle back on Twentymile Loop Trail.

Mile 5.2 Finish.

Hiking Directions

Begin Walk past the gate and onto Twentymile Trail.

Mile 0.6 Turn left on Wolf Ridge Trail and cross the footbridge.

Mile 1.7 Twentymile Loop Trail exits here on the right. Stay on Wolf Ridge Trail.

Mile 2.5 Turn left on the spur trail that leads to campsite #95.

Mile 2.6 Reach campsite #95, named for Dalton Branch, the small thrashing brook that runs through the site. This is a very nice site with space for 8 or 10 tents. It's a great place to while away an afternoon. Dalton Branch

Look for carpets of trout lily on the Twentymile Loop in April.

Twentymile Map

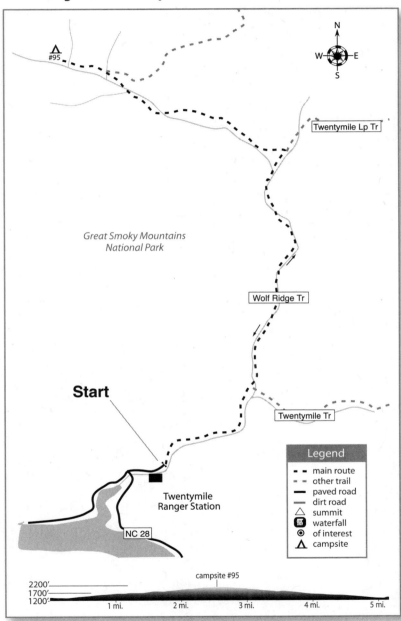

Legend

- - - main route
- - - other trail
— paved road
— dirt road
△ summit
♨ waterfall
◉ of interest
▲ campsite

△ #95

Twentymile Lp Tr

Great Smoky Mountains National Park

Wolf Ridge Tr

Start

Twentymile Tr

Twentymile Ranger Station

NC 28

campsite #95

2200'
1700'
1200'
1 mi.   2 mi.   3 mi.   4 mi.   5 mi.

Gregory Bald

Difficulty	Strenuous
Hike Distance	16 miles
Type of Hike	Loop
Total Ascent	3,800 ft
Land Manager	NPS
Fee	$4 pp pn

pp=per person pn=per night

Gregory Bald overlooks Cades Cove in Tennessee to the north.

An overnight trip over Gregory Bald is great most any time of year, but if you can swing it, make the trek in mid-June. All over the top of the bald grow wild flame azalea. This tall shrub blooms a bright orange, and at this elevation the display is magnificent.

Regardless of when you make your trip, you'll enjoy this remarkable destination. The view from the top is stunning. If you camp at site #13, you're likely to have the place to yourself late in the day and first thing in the morning; most day hikers will arrive around lunchtime, when you're long gone. You may even be tempted to grab your headlamp and a hot drink and head up to the bald for the sunset or sunrise. Either would make the trip that much more memorable.

From the top of the bald, your hike will be almost entirely downhill on a relatively gentle grade. This is good for the knees and for the psyche as well; the miles will breeze by.

Gregory Bald (cont.)

Getting to the Trailhead

From the bridge on NC 28 that crosses Lake Cheoah just below Fontana Dam, travel 5.4 miles to the Twentymile Ranger Station. Trailhead parking is just beyond the office.

GPS Coordinates
N 35° 28.04' W 83° 52.60'

Hiking Directions

Begin Walk around the gate and up Twentymile Trail.

Mile 0.6 Turn left on Wolf Ridge Trail.

Mile 1.7 Twentymile Loop Trail enters from the right. Bear left to stay on Wolf Ridge Trail.

Mile 2.5 A spur trail turns left here to campsite #95, a good option if you get a late start or are making this trip more than two days. This beautiful site has space enough for about 8 tents, with water from a nearby stream. Continue on Wolf Ridge Trail.

Mile 6.1 A long climb culminates at the top of Parson Bald and a tangle of blueberry bushes.

Mile 6.9 Reach campsite #13 in Sheep Pen Gap at 4,600 feet. This high campsite remains cool throughout the summer and is the closest to the summit of Gregory Bald, where you can hike up for a sunset or sunrise. A small seep spring is 100 yards or so down the Gregory Bald Trail. To continue the route, turn right on Gregory Bald Trail.

Mile 7.3 Summit Gregory Bald, with 360-degree views. A magnificent display of flame azalea blooms in mid-June. It's pretty much all downhill from here to the trailhead.

Mile 8.0 Gregory Ridge Trail exits left. Continue straight.

Mile 8.1 Turn right on Long Hungry Ridge Trail.

Mile 11.4 Drop down into campsite #92. This pretty site has plenty of room to spread out and is an ideal spot for a second night on the trail or for ambitious one-nighters. Water is from the adjacent creek.

Mile 12.5 Twentymile Loop Trail exits hard right. Turn right on Twentymile Trail and follow it to the finish.

Mile 13.8 Reach campsite #93, a small campsite right on the creek and another option for a second night. Water is available from the creek.

Mile 15.3 Bear left as you complete the loop.

Mile 16.0 Finish.

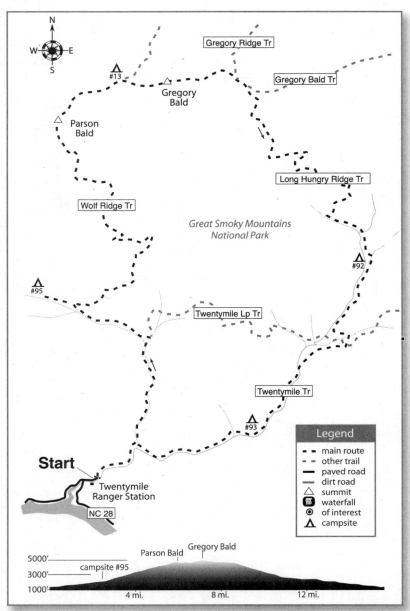

Nantahala National Forest

Contact Information

Cheoah Ranger District
1070 Massey Branch Rd.
Robbinsville, NC 28771
828-479-6431
www.fs.usda.gov/nfsnc
(hikes pp. 77-93)

Nantahala Ranger District
90 Sloan Rd.
Franklin, NC 28734
828-524-6441
www.fs.usda.gov/nfsnc
(hikes pp. 94-122)

Permit Required	No
Fee	None
Max Group Size	See below
Pets Allowed	Yes

pp=per person pn=per night

The Nantahala National Forest covers over half a million acres in far western North Carolina, sharing some of its borders with Tennessee, Georgia, and South Carolina. Backcountry trails within it follow routes across designated wilderness areas, along rushing mountain rivers, past waterfalls, through deep valleys, and over mile-high ridges. You'll find most trails easy to navigate with well-marked signs or blazes, but some which see light use—or which cross designated wilderness where navigation can be more difficult—may not be blazed or marked, making it a challenge in some places to find the tread. In this book, such trails are identified in the route description.

Generally, backcountry regulations follow rather lenient rules, but there are specific guidelines for groups. When hiking in the Joyce Kilmer-Slickrock Wilderness (hikes pp. 77-89), maximum group size is 10 people. Hikers traveling through the Chattooga River Wild and Scenic corridor (hikes pp. 110-112) should limit their groups to 12 people. And if you plan to take a group to Panthertown Valley (hikes pp. 103-109), camping groups are limited to 12 people per site.

Slickrock Creek

Difficulty	Strenuous
Hike Distance	14.3 miles
Type of Hike	Loop
Total Ascent	4,900 ft
Land Manager	USFS
Fee	None

Lower Falls on Slickrock Creek is a fabulous spot to relax and enjoy the water.

Make no mistake, this is a difficult hike and not a good choice after heavy rainfall. Slickrock Creek drains a large watershed and can quickly turn from a pretty mountain stream into a raging torrent. After six miles of relatively short and steep ups and downs, the route *finally* reaches Slickrock Creek. The next six miles takes you back and forth across the creek more than a dozen times where in places the stream is waist deep. In other spots you're forced to hang on to bare rock walls as you tiptoe along mere inches from the water. Finally, near the end of the hike, you'll find yourself holding your breath as you cross rough wooden bridges along cliffs or cling to roots to avoid slipping into the abyss.

Why, you might ask, would anyone want to take an overnight trip here? Come on, it's a great hike! Campsites are plentiful along Slickrock Creek. You'll see two major waterfalls. You're in the Joyce Kilmer–Slickrock Wilderness. There are huge swimming holes; the fishing is awesome. Everything—the woods, the wildflowers, the creek—is just beautiful. If you're up for the challenge, you'll have a great and memorable time.

Slickrock Creek (cont.)

Getting to the Trailhead

From the traffic light in Robbinsville, travel 15.5 miles north on US 129. You'll cross the Cheoah River below Tapoco. At Cheoah Dam, just before crossing a second bridge, turn left down the short road to the trailhead. Additional parking is across the bridge at the campground.

GPS Coordinates

N 35° 26.93' W 83° 56.47'

Hiking Directions

Begin Walk out along the lake on Slickrock Creek Trail. This is also Benton MacKaye Trail here.

Mile 0.6 Turn left on Ike Branch Trail.

Mile 2.2 Reach Yellowhammer Gap and a trail junction. Hangover Lead Trail exits toward the gap to the left and meets Belding Trail. Continue straight on Ike Branch Trail.

Mile 2.3 Bear left on Yellow Hammer Trail. This trail skirts the side of the mountain, dipping to

cross small streams, then climbing steeply over the next shoulder, all the while gradually heading down the mountain. For a much shorter loop, you could continue on Ike Branch Trail down to Slickrock Creek.

Mile 4.0 Reach an old homesite. You'll see remnants of a stone wall, an old chimney, and a small family cemetery. This is a good campsite if you are staying out for more than one night. Water is from an adjacent stream. Turn left here on Nichols Cove Trail. You could also shortcut the route here by turning right.

Mile 5.0 Climb steeply to Windy Gap, where Windy Gap Trail enters from the left. Continue over the gap, staying on Nichols Cove Trail.

Mile 5.7 Reach junction with Big Fat Gap Trail. Slickrock Creek is just ahead, as are several options for camping. You'll find campsites on either side of Big Fat Branch as it enters Slickrock Creek and another site on the far side of Slickrock Creek.If these don't appeal to you, there are many more to choose from up ahead. To continue on this route, you'll need to ford Slickrock Creek here. Get used to it; there are 12 more crossings to go as you follow Slickrock Creek Trail for the remainder of the hike.

Mile 6.0 More campsites can be found here at this crossing.

Mile 6.6 Big Stack Gap Trail exits left.

Mile 6.8 You'll find a large campsite here. It's the closest one to Wildcat Falls.

Mile 7.0 Just below this crossing is Wildcat Falls, made up of four waterfalls in quick succession for a total drop of around 60 feet.

Mile 8.7 The trail here hugs the rocks along the left side of the creek. It's a tight spot.

Mile 9.7 Nichols Cove Trail exits here right.

Mile 9.9 Stiff Knee Trail (no doubt how it got that name!) exits left here as Benton MacKaye Trail rejoins your route. There are good campsites here as well.

Mile 10.5 Ike Branch Trail enters here from the right. This is another area of nice campsites. Just below is a dicey section where the trail hugs the rocks just above the creek for a short distance.

Mile 11.1 Here the trail comes down from high above the creek to a very nice campsite. This is the nearest site to Lower Falls.

Mile 11.2 Reach Lower Falls, which drops 20 feet into a huge plungepool—great for swimming in warm weather.

Mile 11.8 For the next tenth of a mile you'll need to skirt wide right around a washout area and then hug the base of a cliff just above the creek to continue on the trail.

Mile 12.5 Start looking for the trail to turn right up and away from the creek. If you reach the lake, you've gone too far! The next mile or so of trail is technically difficult. Watch for steep

dropoffs, creaky wooden bridges, and loose sections where you'll need to cling to roots as you make your way high above the lake below.

Mile 13.7 The trail settles down now as you close the loop.

Mile 14.3 Finish.

Rough wooden bridges are suspended over cliff faces on this challenging section of trail.

Slickrock Creek Map

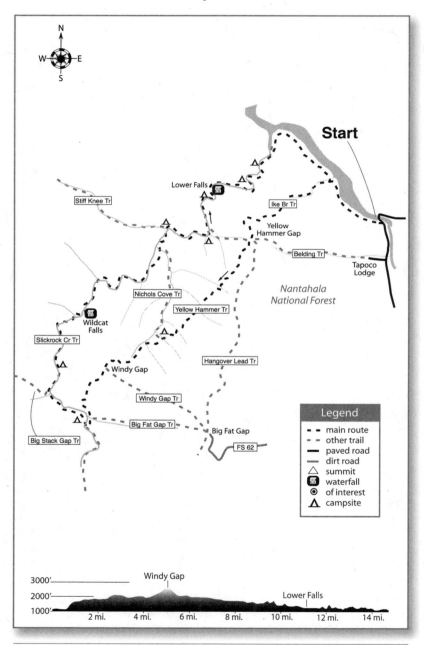

Joyce Kilmer

Difficulty	Easier
Hike Distance	1-6 miles
Type of Hike	Out & Back
Total Ascent	1,400 ft
Land Manager	USFS
Fee	None

You'll see more trees like this giant poplar on this overnight hike in Joyce Kilmer.

Big trees are the main attraction of this overnight trip. Folks come from far and wide to stand in the huge old-growth forest of Joyce Kilmer. Although camping is prohibited in the Memorial Forest itself, you can still spend a night out among some giants nearby.

There is something about hiking into the forest of Joyce Kilmer that makes you tread along in silence. It's like walking into church. You nod your head occasionally, you might whisper a hello to a passing fellow hiker, but mostly you just walk along in quiet reverence for the supreme beings all around you. It calms your spirit and welcomes you back again and again.

You can make this trip from one to six miles long, depending on where you want to spend the night, so it's a perfect trip for a first-time overnight with a youngster. There are several good campsites to choose from, all close to the creek, and you can always make a detour into the Memorial section to see classic virgin forest.

Getting to the Trailhead

From the traffic light in Robbinsville, drive north on US 129 for 8.2 miles. Turn left on Joyce Kilmer Road and continue another 6 miles to the entrance to Joyce Kilmer Memorial Forest. Continue another 0.5 mile to the trailhead to drop off gear and people. No overnight parking is allowed here, so you'll need to return your car to the parking spot near the beginning of the entrance road.

GPS Coordinates

N 35° 21.52' W 83° 55.72'

Hiking Directions

Begin Walk out past the information station and onto the combined Naked Ground and Joyce Kilmer Memorial Loop Trails.

Mile 0.2 Bear right on Naked Ground Trail as JK Memorial Loop heads off to the left.

Mile 0.5 Naked Ground Connector Trail enters from the right. Stay straight on Naked Ground

Trail and then bear right as the trail splits into lower and upper trails. Go left here to the first campsite. It's a good one, with room for 3 to 4 tents right on the creek. If you decide to move on, go right instead of left to continue.

Mile 1.6 Here you'll reach the second campsite, a small one with room for just 1 or 2 tents. Water is from the adjacent creek.

Mile 2.2 A very small campsite here has room for one tent. Another (just barely larger) site is located a little farther along. Water is from the adjacent creek.

Mile 3.0 After hiking through an area of very large trees, you'll reach the last campsite before the trail begins to climb steeply toward Naked Ground. This is a relatively small site with space for just a few tents. Water is from the adjacent creek. Whichever site you choose, return to the trailhead the same way you came in.

Mile 6.0 Finish.

Vassey's Trillium is a common sight in spring at Joyce Kilmer.

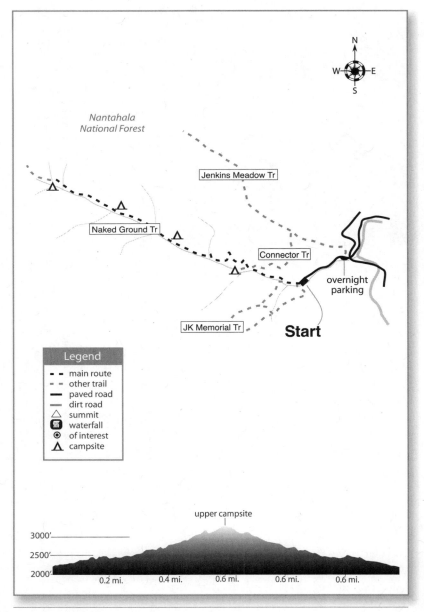

Naked Ground Hangover

Difficulty	Moderate
Hike Distance	12 miles
Type of Hike	Loop
Total Ascent	4,140 ft
Land Manager	USFS
Fee	None

At Naked Ground there is a major trail junction with trails going in all directions.

Have you ever wanted to watch the sunrise from your sleeping bag? If you're fortunate enough to get the right tent site up at Naked Ground, your wish could be granted. This popular destination in Joyce Kilmer–Slickrock Wilderness Area is high on the list of must-dos for anyone backpacking in the North Carolina mountains.

Your overnight tramp starts at the entrance to the Joyce Kilmer Memorial Forest where old-growth tulip poplars and hemlocks tower over the land. You won't hike through the Memorial Forest proper, but on your way up Naked Ground Trail you'll pass underneath some monsters. The last mile or so before reaching Naked Ground is pretty steep, but the switchbacks make it bearable, and regardless of where you actually set up shelter, your night out here will be memorable.

Day two begins with a slight climb up toward Hangover Lead, where you definitely will want to detour over to the "hangover" for the amazing 360-degree view before coasting back down the mountain, out of the wilderness and eventually back to civilization.

Getting to the Trailhead

From the traffic light in Robbinsville, drive north on US 129 for 8.2 miles. Turn left on Joyce Kilmer Road and continue another 6.0 miles to the entrance to Joyce Kilmer Memorial Forest. Park here at the Jenkins Meadow Trailhead immediately on the left. Overnight parking is not allowed at the Joyce Kilmer Memorial Trailhead.

GPS Coordinates
N 35° 21.74′ W 83° 55.29′

Hiking Directions

Begin Walk along the pavement for the first half-mile.

Mile 0.5 Continue out past the information station and onto the combined Naked Ground and Joyce Kilmer Memorial Loop Trails.

Mile 0.8 Bear right on Naked Ground Trail as JK Memorial Loop heads off to the left.

Mile 1.1 Naked Ground Connector Trail enters from the right.

Stay straight on Naked Ground Trail, then bear right as the trail splits into lower and upper trails. There is a good campsite just down the left split if you are in need of one.

Mile 2.2 Here you'll reach the second campsite, a small one with room for 1 or 2 tents. Water is from the adjacent creek.

Mile 2.5 A very small campsite here has room for a single tent. Another (just barely larger) site is located a little farther along. Water is from the adjacent creek.

Mile 3.9 After hiking through an area of very large trees, you'll reach the last campsite before the trail begins to climb steeply toward Naked Ground. This is a relatively small site just big enough for a few tents. Water is from the adjacent creek.

Mile 5.7 Reach Naked Ground, a major trail intersection and your best bet for a campsite. It comes complete with an awesome view facing east. Yes, you can watch the sunrise from your sleeping bag! Water is from a small spring 100 paces down Slickrock Creek Trail. Turn right onto Haoe Lead Trail.

Mile 6.6 This is the high point of the hike. Turn left on Hangover Lead Trail for the short detour out to the "hangover."

Mile 7.0 Deep Creek Trail will enter from the right, and then the trail opens up in a high meadow with several dry campsites just beyond it. A little farther on you'll reach the "hangover." Enjoy one

Naked Ground (cont.)

of the best views in this wilderness area, then return to the high point and turn left to continue on Haoe Lead Trail.

Mile 8.6 Turn right on Jenkins Meadow Trail, which leads down the mountain.

Mile 11.0 Naked Ground Connector Trail exits right. Stay straight on Jenkins Meadow Trail.

Mile 12.0 Finish where your car is parked in the overnight lot.

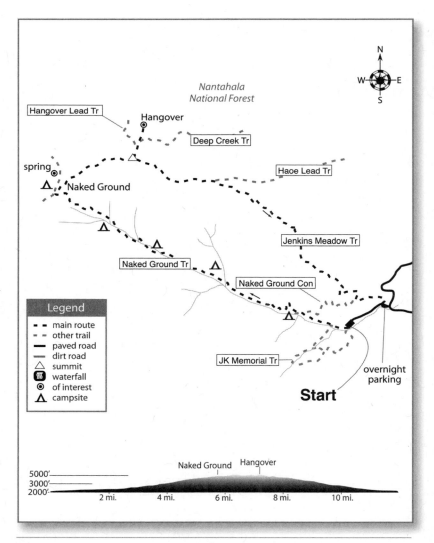

Stratton Bald

Difficulty	Strenuous
Hike Distance	13.8 miles
Type of Hike	Loop
Total Ascent	4,276 ft
Land Manager	USFS
Fee	None

You'll get a good view of Stratton Bald partway through your hike.

This route is rated strenuous due to a long climb on a rugged trail. Some sections are steep, and in a few places where vegetation is creeping back onto the foot path, the trail may be hard to see. Also, water is all but nonexistent along the high, dry ridges until you reach a small spring at Naked Ground, which is your best option for a campsite. The views along the way are fantastic.

You'll be in the Joyce Kilmer–Slickrock Wilderness for almost the entire route. You may have read that trails in designated wilderness areas are unsigned, unblazed, and unmaintained. The reality is that in much of the Southeast, designated wilderness trails often do have signs at intersections, and typically are in good shape. Rarely do you see blazes, but route-finding is not nearly as difficult as you might have thought. Still, in no way does this hike resemble a walk in your neighborhood park. Amenities are just what nature provides, and you are about as far out in the boonies as it's possible to get.

Stratton Bald (cont.)

Getting to the Trailhead

From the traffic light in Robbinsville, drive north on US 129 for 8.2 miles. Turn left on Joyce Kilmer Road and continue another 6.0 miles to the entrance to Joyce Kilmer Memorial Forest. Park here at the Jenkins Meadow Trailhead immediately on the left.

GPS Coordinates

N 35° 21.74' W 83° 55.29'

Hiking Directions

Begin Walk on the road back to the entrance and turn right.

Mile 0.3 Just before crossing Santeetla Creek, turn right on Stratton Bald Trail.

Mile 2.9 Reach a gap where you'll find a ridgetop campsite. There is no water source. Continue on with steady climbing. The next stretch can be a bit overgrown, especially in summer.

Mile 4.0 The views to the south really open up here. You may

hear motorcycles on the Cherohala Skyway across the valley.

Mile 5.3 An unmarked trail exits left at a gap. Bear right.

Mile 5.5 Wolf Laurel Trail exits left and heads toward Swann Cabin. Stay right on Stratton Bald Trail.

Mile 6.6 On a lonely, rocky spine, Haoe Lead Trail turns off to the right. You'll return to this spot, but for now turn left to walk up to Stratton Bald.

Mile 7.8 Reach Stratton Bald the highlight of the trip. There are great views to be had from this open meadow. Turn back to the Haoe Lead Trail junction, where you'll go left.

Mile 8.6 Reach Naked Ground and the best campsite on this route. You'll find water at a spring 100 paces down Slickrock Creek Trail. Enjoy the view and your night out. When you leave here, turn right on Naked Ground Trail and head down the mountain.

Mile 10.3 Pass a small campsite down by the creek. This can be a good alternative if the Naked Ground site is full.

Mile 11.0 Pass a couple of small campsites on the creek.

Mile 11.7 Pass the last possible campsite before reaching the Memorial Forest.

Mile 13.3 Reach the Memorial Forest trailhead. Walk the road back to your car.

Mile 13.8 Finish.

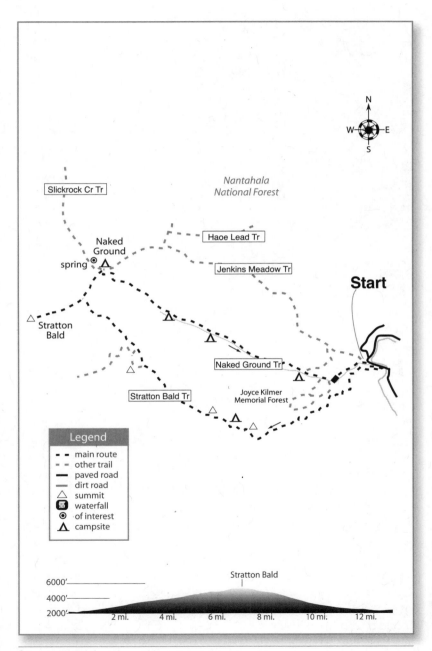

Start

Slickrock Cr Tr

Nantahala
National Forest

Naked
Ground

spring

Haoe Lead Tr

Jenkins Meadow Tr

Stratton
Bald

Naked Ground Tr

Joyce Kilmer
Memorial Forest

Stratton Bald Tr

Legend
- - - main route
- - - other trail
— paved road
— dirt road
△ summit
🌊 waterfall
◉ of interest
▲ campsite

Stratton Bald

6000'
4000'
2000'
2 mi.   4 mi.   6 mi.   8 mi.   10 mi.   12 mi.

Nantahala National Forest: Joyce Kilmer–Slickrock Wilderness Area

Big Snowbird

Difficulty	Strenuous
Hike Distance	13.2 miles
Type of Hike	Loop
Total Ascent	3,250 ft
Land Manager	USFS
Fee	None

This is the only bridge on Snowbird Creek.
You'll get wet feet at all other crossings.

This is the kind of hike that makes you curse the guidebook author when you're struggling through a rhododendron thicket, unsure if you are even on the trail! If the Burntrock Ridge Trail ever became maintained—or even more often used—this hike would not be rated nearly as difficult. As it is, you'll want to be super-confident in your wilderness navigation skills, give yourself lots of time, and keep an eye on the weather. This is not a trail to hike in a rainstorm or when the creek is in flood, as you'd never get across safely.

Sound too difficult? Don't be discouraged. It's a great place for an overnight trip. You'll see four different waterfalls. If it's warm, the swimming is fantastic. Do you like to fish for trout? The creek is pristine and the fishing is awesome. Do you like wildflowers? The woods are full of them.

Starting out, things seem easy as you walk along an old railroad grade above Snowbird Creek. Once you leave Sassafras Falls, the going gets tougher as you work through tangles of rhododendron and try to locate a "barely there" trail. Once back on Big Snowbird you can relax.

Getting to the Trailhead

From the traffic light in Robbinsville, take US 129 north for 1.4 miles and turn left on NC 143. Continue 5.7 miles and turn left on Snowbird Road. Continue 2.1 miles and make a very hard left to stay on Snowbird Road. Go another 1.0 mile and turn right on Big Snowbird Road. After another 2.1 miles the road turns to gravel and becomes FS 75. You'll reach the trailhead in an additional 3.9 miles.

GPS Coordinates
N 35° 15.87' W 83° 56.28'

Hiking Directions

Begin From the trailhead, take the left-most trail up and around the gate. Big Snowbird Trail follows an old railroad grade, making for fairly easy walking.

Mile 1.5 Reach the first good campsite down on the flats beside the creek. There is plenty of

room here. Water is from Snowbird Creek.

Mile 2.3 Pass a pipe spring, a good source of water should you need any.

Mile 2.5 Reach a second and smaller campsite. Water is from a stream you'll need to cross to continue the route.

Mile 2.9 After climbing a hill, turn hard back to the left on Sassafras Creek Trail. It may or may not be marked.

Mile 3.6 A side trail on the left leads to a view of Sassafras Falls, an 80-foot tiered waterfall. You may want to leave your pack here for the scramble down to the falls. The trail continues up past the brink of the waterfall.

Mile 4.0 You'll find a small campsite by the creek here. If you're out for two nights, this is a good choice before heading up

Middle Falls has a nice plungepool at the bottom.

into the more difficult-to-navigate section of trail. To continue you'll need to turn right here, away from the creek. Look for a distinct but little-used path heading up a draw. You may see a ribbon on a tree to mark the way. This path is the Burntrock Ridge Trail. It climbs up the draw through tangles of rhododendron to a ridge. At the crest of the ridge turn left and follow the spine rather steeply for a short distance before it levels off somewhat.

Mile 5.0 It gets trickier. Be on the lookout for a faint path angling off the ridge to the right. If you're lucky, you'll spot bits of survey ribbon which act as confidence markers. At times the trail is obvious; at others, it's little more than a game trail. The farther you go down the mountain, the more distinct it becomes.

Mile 5.6 Reach Little Flat Creek. Bear right as the trail follows the creek downstream.

Mile 5.8 Turn left on Big Snowbird Creek Trail. Congratulations! You've made it through the hard-to-navigate section.

Mile 6.0 Reach an area of campsites. There is one here and another a little farther along on the same side of Snowbird Creek. Either is a good choice if you want a spot from which to explore the upper waterfalls. Upper Falls is 0.8 mile upstream, and Middle Falls is 0.5 mile downstream. Regardless of what you do, you'll need to ford the creek here, as the trail continues on the other side. The following mileage assumes you hiked up to Upper Falls.

Mile 6.8 Upper Falls, a 20-foot slide into a nice pool, is the turn-around point for this route.

Mile 7.6 Back at the stream ford, across from the campsite, turn left (away from the creek) on Middle Falls Trail.

Mile 7.9 Turn right on a spur trail leading to Middle Falls.

Mile 8.1 Reach Middle Falls, a 20-foot-high, 50-foot-wide block waterfall dropping into a very large plungepool. Return to Middle Falls Trail the way you came and continue on it as it diverges up and over a spine well away from Snowbird Creek.

Mile 9.3 Turn left as you rejoin Big Snowbird Trail. The very nice campsite here is a good choice if making this a two-night hike.

Mile 9.6 A steep side trail leads down to where you can see a small portion of Big Falls. You can certainly hear it up on the trail.

Mile 10.5 Close the loop as you reach the turn off of Sassafras Trail. Continue on Big Snowbird Trail back to the trailhead.

Mile 13.2 Finish.

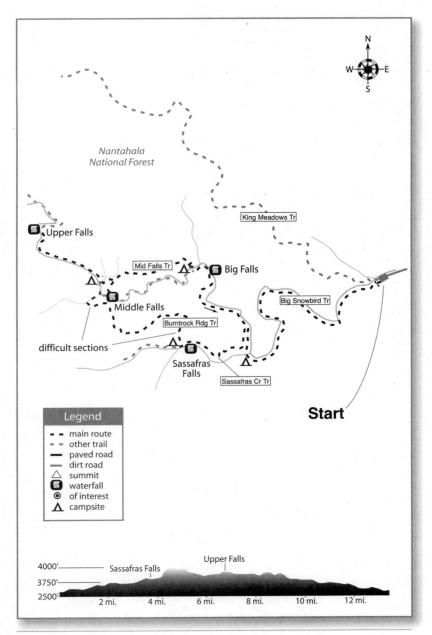

Nantahala
National Forest

King Meadows Tr

Upper Falls

Mid Falls Tr

Big Falls

Middle Falls

Big Snowbird Tr

Burntrock Rdg Tr

difficult sections

Sassafras
Falls

Sassafras Cr Tr

Start

Legend

- - main route
- - - other trail
— paved road
— dirt road
△ summit
▨ waterfall
◉ of interest
▲ campsite

4000' — Sassafras Falls   Upper Falls
3750' —
2500' —

2 mi.   4 mi.   6 mi.   8 mi.   10 mi.   12 mi.

Wesser Bald Tower

Difficulty	Moderate
Hike Distance	11 miles
Type of Hike	Loop
Total Ascent	3,280 ft
Land Manager	USFS
Fee	None

Climb to the viewing platform atop Wesser Bald Tower for a 360-degree view.

This is the only hike in the book that requires either two vehicles for a shuttle or getting someone to drop you off at the start. Since the route finishes at the Nantahala Outdoor Center, chances are you won't have much trouble arranging for someone from there to drop you off at the trailhead if you need it.

Hiking up to Wesser Bald Tower is great fun. Originally the tower supported—as did most such towers—a structure with glass windows all the way around from which fire lookouts watched vigilantly for telltale smoke for days at a time. Very few of the original towers remain, but fortunately for hikers, a platform has replaced the little house at the top of the Wesser Bald Tower, providing a 360-degree view.

On this route you'll camp at the Wesser Bald Shelter on the Appalachian Trail. From the shelter it's a two-mile round trip hike to the tower and back, which makes a nice walk, especially since you can leave your pack behind. Day two is entirely on the AT, ending up at the Nantahala River where you can eat and shop right on the river at NOC.

Getting to the Trailhead

From Nantahala Outdoor Center, 13.0 miles west of Bryson City, drive east on US 74 for 0.9 mile. Turn right on Wesser Creek Road and drive to the trailhead at the end of the road, 1.9 more miles. If you have two vehicles, leave one at NOC where the hike ends, or you may be able to arrange a shuttle through the NOC Outfitter Store (828-488-2175).

GPS Coordinates

N 35° 18.30′ W 83° 34.68′

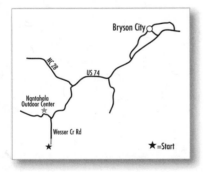

Hiking Directions

Begin Walk out the back of the parking lot on Wesser Creek Trail.

Mile 3.2 A steady climb brings you to the Appalachian Trail. Just across the trail is a shelter and your home for tonight. There's room for 4 to 5 folks in the shelter, or you can set up a tent out front. The water source is a pipespring 0.2 mile from, and just off to the left of, the AT toward the tower. You can set up camp and then head on up to Wesser Bald Tower for the views; it's a mile up and another back. If this site is full, there is another small campsite beyond the spring on the AT. After your night out and a visit to the tower, continue on the AT heading north.

Mile 6.5 The AT descends through a notch in a cliff. The view is good from here.

Mile 9.8 Reach the Rufus Morgan Shelter. This site is very popular due to its proximity to NOC. It has room for tents down nearer the creek, which serves as the water source.

Mile 11.0 Finish at NOC.

It's fun to read the logbooks commonly found in AT shelters.

Wesser Bald Tower Map

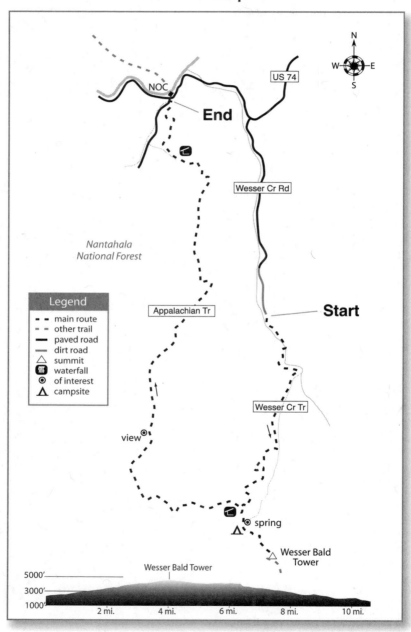

US 74

NOC

End

Wesser Cr Rd

Nantahala
National Forest

Appalachian Tr

Start

Legend
- - - main route
- - other trail
—— paved road
—— dirt road
△ summit
▨ waterfall
◉ of interest
▲ campsite

Wesser Cr Tr

view ◉

spring

Wesser Bald
Tower

Wesser Bald Tower

5000'
3000'
1000'

2 mi.   4 mi.   6 mi.   8 mi.   10 mi.

Standing Indian Mountain

Difficulty	Moderate
Hike Distance	11.4 miles
Type of Hike	Loop
Total Ascent	2,540 ft
Land Manager	USFS
Fee	None

Southbounders enjoying their last 5,000- foot view from atop Standing Indian Mountain.

Overnight hikes along the Appalachian Trail are always fun. There is such an aura attached to the AT—even though on this trip you're not hiking all the way to Maine, the possibility still exists. You step onto the trail and magically you're transported into the world of the AT, where hikers have special trail names and you sleep out in the woods every night for months on end. You'll imagine what it must feel like to make such a commitment—to hike the entire thing. You strike up conversations with fellow hikers, and often the question comes up, "Are you hiking *all the way*?"

This route in Standing Indian is a great AT introduction. You'll have the opportunity to spend the night at a shelter (one of over 250 between Georgia and Maine), and you'll summit the first 5,000-foot-high mountain AT northbounders encounter. It has a great view into Georgia. Like many hikes in this guide, the first day is mostly uphill (not too steep in this case) and the second is mostly down (pretty steep in places; trekking poles are recommended). After the 11-plus miles are finished, chances are you'll be plotting a way to take six months off and do the whole thing.

Standing Indian Mountain (cont.)

Getting to the Trailhead

From the intersection of US 64 and US 441 in Franklin, travel 12 miles on US 64. Turn left on W. Old Murphy Road. Drive 1.9 miles and turn right toward the Standing Indian Campground. Continue another 2.1 miles to the trailhead and park next to the backcountry information kiosk.

GPS Coordinates
N 35° 04.49' W 83° 31.63'

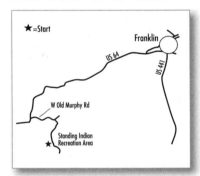

Hiking Directions

Begin Walk out the blue-blazed trail leading toward all other trails.

Mile 0.1 Enter the campground and turn left on the road shoulder, cross the Nantahala River on a bridge, and turn right at the sign for Kimsey Creek Trail and several other trails.

Mile 0.3 Turn left on blue-blazed Kimsey Creek Trail.

Mile 0.7 An old forest road enters from the left. The trail bears right on this old roadbed.

Mile 1.0 Reach a campsite on the right which, if you got a late start, could be a possiblity. Water is from Kimsey Creek. You'll turn left here past a gate to continue on Kimsey Creek Trail.

Mile 1.2 Connector Trail exits right. Stay on Kimsey Creek Trail.

Mile 2.0 Cross Kimsey Creek on a footbridge and soon reach the second campsite of 4 within the first 4 miles. Water from creek.

Mile 3.1 Reach the third campsite, a small one by the creek.

Mile 3.5 Junction with FS 7219. Go left on the road, pass the gate, and then right back onto the foot trail. Look for blue blazes.

Mile 4.2 Reach a medium-sized campsite (room for 4 tents). Water is from a small branch next to the site. You are very close to a trailhead at the end of FS 7219.

Mile 4.3 Reach the trailhead. Turn left on the Appalachian Trail.

Mile 5.0 Reach a small campsite atop a ridge. Water is from a creek down a steep hill.

Mile 5.2 First you should see a blue-blazed trail on the left (leads to water source) and then a trail on the right which leads back to a trail shelter. This is your best bet for camping. It's a small shelter which accommodates 4 or 5 folks. Behind it is room for a few tents. From the shelter, you have a view of Standing Indian Mountain through the trees. After your night out, continue on the AT and your climb up Standing Indian Mountain.

Mile 6.9 Lower Ridge Trail exits left here. This is your turn, but first take a right to walk up to the summit of Standing Indian Mountain.

Mile 7.0 Reach the summit where you have a fantastic view from a small clearing. Return to the AT and take Lower Ridge Trail down the mountain.

Mile 10.9 Back in the campground, follow the route across the bridge, then right to return to where you started.

Mile 11.4 Finish.

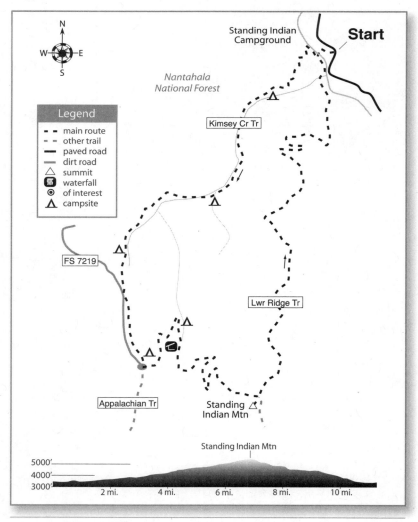

Whiteoak Stamp

You can recognize the yellow birch tree by its shiny, peeling bark.

Difficulty	Easier
Hike Distance	8 miles
Type of Hike	Out & Back
Total Ascent	1,400 ft
Land Manager	USFS
Fee	None

For those in the know, this is an exciting hike. You'll walk up to Whiteoak Stamp, a place of great biological diversity. It's classified as a "special interest area" by the U.S. Forest Service. Here you'll see a forest of northern red oak and giant old yellow birches located on what for such a high elevation is relatively level ground. Your night out will be at Muskrat Creek Shelter, a nice spot on the edge of the stamp—a place where livestock traditionally driven into the high country to graze in summer congregated and stamped the ground flat. You can stay in the shelter or camp outside at one of several level spots.

On day two, you'll detour onto the old Appalachian Trail to explore the edge of a rare high-altitude heath bog. It's not much to look at unless you know what you are seeing; the rhododendron, mountain laurel, and flame azalea are thick as the dickens. But somewhere in that impenetrable jungle are water courses and an open sedge marsh, home to the endangered bog turtle. Explore around here as much as you like before looping back to the AT by way of Chunky Gal Trail.

Getting to the Trailhead

From the intersection of US 64 and US 441 in Franklin, travel 14.7 miles on US 64. Turn left at the brown sign for FS 71 and Deep Gap. Follow FS 71 5.9 single-lane twisting dirt miles to the Deep Gap trailhead at the end of the road.

Note: FS 71 is closed from January 1 to April 1.

GPS Coordinates

N 35° 02.37′ W 83° 33.15′

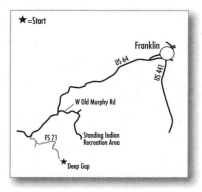

Hiking Directions

Begin Walk south on the Appalachian Trail as it loops around and gradually climbs the flanks of Yellow Mountain.

Mile 2.1 Reach Wateroak Gap. Stay straight on the AT.

Mile 2.9 Chunky Gal Trail exits here to the right. Stay on the AT.

Mile 3.2 Reach White Oak Stamp sign. You've actually been in the stamp for a while.

Mile 4.0 Look left just before crossing a small stream for Muskrat Creek Shelter. This is your camping spot for tonight. There is room for five or six hikers in the shelter, or you can camp out front or in back at one of the small level spots. There is a privy here as well as a picnic table under the shelter roof. Water is obtained from the adjacent small stream. After your night out, return in the direction you came.

Mile 4.8 Back at the White Oak Stamp sign, detour left on the old unmarked AT.

Mile 4.9 The dense tangle of shrubs to your left marks the edge of the heath bog. It's pretty darn thick in there.

Mile 5.0 Make a hard right turn onto Chunky Gal Trail and climb back up to the AT.

Mile 5.2 Turn left to continue back to the trailhead on the AT.

Mile 8.0 Finish.

When you reach this sign, you know you're in the stamp.

Whiteoak Stamp Map

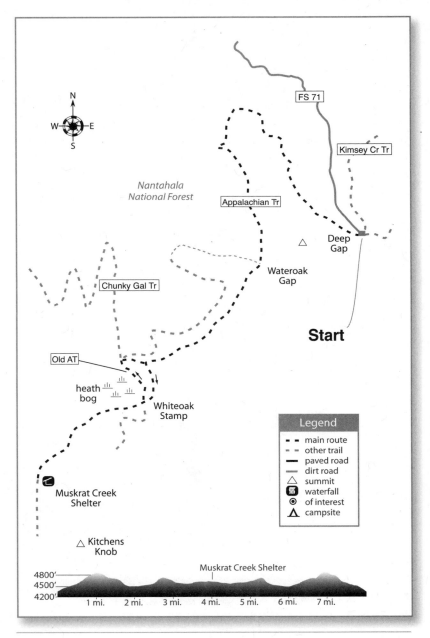

FS 71

Kimsey Cr Tr

N
W — E
S

*Nantahala
National Forest*

Appalachian Tr

Deep
Gap

Wateroak
Gap

Chunky Gal Tr

Start

Old AT

heath
bog

Whiteoak
Stamp

Legend
- – – main route
- - - - other trail
- —— paved road
- —— dirt road
- △ summit
- ⬚ waterfall
- ⊙ of interest
- ▲ campsite

Muskrat Creek
Shelter

△ Kitchens
Knob

Muskrat Creek Shelter

4800'
4500'
4200'
1 mi. 2 mi. 3 mi. 4 mi. 5 mi. 6 mi. 7 mi.

Panthertown Valley

You can see the Great Wall of Big Green Mountain as you hike into the valley.

Difficulty	Easier
Hike Distance	4.7 miles
Type of Hike	Loop
Total Ascent	500 ft
Land Manager	USFS
Fee	None

For years Panthertown Valley was a little-known hidden gem up on the Highlands Plateau. Protected from development by owner Duke Power, in 1989 it became a part of the Nantahala National Forest. Now hikers, rock climbers, mountain bikers, and birders regularly frequent the area, and it's no wonder. Sheer cliffs, rare bogs, waterfalls, and miles of trails make it a real treat for anyone who visits.

This relatively easy route takes you right down to the valley floor where you'll find enjoyable hiking as you circle the boggy area that serves as the headwaters of the Tuckaseegee River. For your night out, there are plenty of camping spots to choose from, all on level ground with plenty of water nearby. Whether you pitch your tent near the bogs and look for rare plants, choose the large trail shelter near Granny Burrell Falls where you can hang out by the creek, or sleep in a more secluded white pine grove, you can't go wrong. Just remember to save enough energy for the climb out of the valley on the second day.

Panthertown Valley (cont.)

Getting to the Trailhead

From the junction of NC 107 and US 64 in Cashiers, drive 2.0 miles east on US 64. Turn left on Cedar Creek Road and go 2.3 miles. Turn right on Breedlove Road and proceed 3.5 miles to its end at Salt Rock Gap trailhead.

GPS Coordinates

N 35° 10.07' W 83° 02.39'

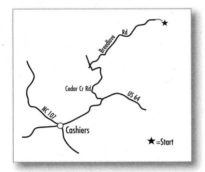

Hiking Directions

Begin Walk around the gate and down Panthertown Valley Trail.

Mile 0.6 Deep Gap Trail enters from the right. Continue on Panthertown Valley Trail.

Mile 0.9 Reach a major trail intersection and the floor of the valley. Continue straight on Panthertown Valley Trail.

Mile 1.6 Turn right and ford the creek. You'll get your feet wet here.

Mile 2.2 Turn right on Macs Gap Trail.

Mile 2.3 Reach a series of excellent campsites on either side of the trail a canopy of white pines. Water is available from adjacent small streams. The trail continues.

Mile 3.0 Turn left on Granny Burrell Falls Trail.

Mile 3.1 Reach Granny Burrell Falls. Below the falls is a large pool, a great place to wade around or just hang out on the large flat rocks.

Mile 3.4 At the junction of Great Wall Trail the route continues to the right, crossing the creek. However, if you're still looking for a campsite, turn left here. Just up ahead is a large trail shelter and a big flat area with room for plenty of tents. Water is available from the adjacent stream.

Mile 3.7 Turn right on Deep Gap Trail.

Mile 3.9 Just off the trail in a grove of white pines is your last campsite option on this hike, a small site for just a few tents. Water is available from the adjacent stream.

Mile 4.0 Turn left on Panthertown Valley Trail and return up the same hill you first hiked down.

Mile 4.7 Finish.

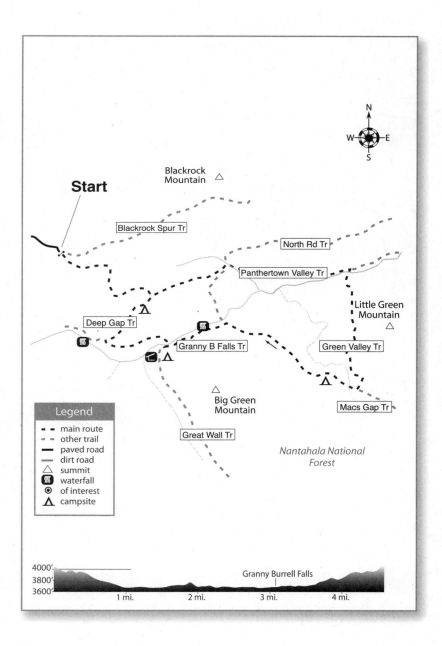

Start

Blackrock
Mountain △

Blackrock Spur Tr

North Rd Tr

Panthertown Valley Tr

Little Green
Mountain
△

Deep Gap Tr

Granny B Falls Tr

Green Valley Tr

Big Green
Mountain
△

Macs Gap Tr

Great Wall Tr

*Nantahala National
Forest*

Legend

- - main route
- - other trail
— paved road
〰〰 dirt road
△ summit
♨ waterfall
⊙ of interest
▲ campsite

4000'
3800'
3600'

Granny Burrell Falls

1 mi.　　2 mi.　　3 mi.　　4 mi.

Panthertown Waterfalls

Difficulty	Moderate
Hike Distance	9.6 miles
Type of Hike	Loop
Total Ascent	1,780 ft
Land Manager	USFS
Fee	None

You'll find 60-foot Wardens Falls hidden in a tangle of rhododendron.

There are at least twelve different waterfalls in Panthertown Valley. On this trek you'll have the chance to visit five or more of them. You'll also walk along the tops of several of the dome-shaped mountains that give this area the nickname "the Yosemite of the East." The views from these high cliffs are amazing.

Hiking to waterfalls is great fun, and every falls is different. Some are high, some are tiered, some land in big plungepools, some slide down the faces of vast rock slabs, some roar so loud it's hard to be heard. As the water crashes into the rocks, positive-charge ions are cast into the air. You literally get "charged up" just being near the waterfall.

Your overnight begins with a hike over Blackrock Mountain for a cliff-top view, then takes you down to a campsite next to Panthertown Creek. From here you can explore a number of waterfalls. Next day you'll hike over Little Green Mountain (more views), then head down below the Great Wall of Big Green Mountain to another beautiful campsite and more waterfalls. You may even decide to stay out an additional night.

Getting to the Trailhead

From the junction of NC 107 and US 64 in Cashiers, drive 2.0 miles east on US 64. Turn left on Cedar Creek Road and go 2.3 miles. Turn right on Breedlove Road and continue 3.5 miles to its end at Salt Rock Gap trailhead.

GPS Coordinates
N 35° 10.07' W 83° 02.39'

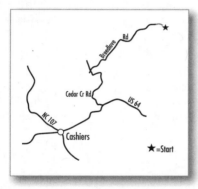

Hiking Directions

Begin Walk between the info board and gate onto Blackrock Spur Trail.

Mile 0.2 Turn right onto Blackrock Trail.

Mile 0.9 Make a right turn onto Overlook Trail.

Mile 1.3 After summiting Blackrock Mountain, you'll arrive at this clifftop overlook. Bear left as the trail skirts the clifftop.

Mile 1.5 Turn right on Powerline Trail.

Mile 2.4 Bear right underneath the powerlines.

Mile 2.6 Look sharp for the first unmarked trail on the left. It looks like a water diversion from the hump in the road. Turn left to descend to Wardens Falls. Farther downstream are Jawbone and Riding Ford Falls. If you plan to stay in the nearby campsite, you may want to continue there and return here after setting up camp.

Mile 2.8 Reach Wardens Falls. After a good look, return to and continue on Powerline Trail.

Mile 3.0 North Road Trail exits to the right. Stay straight.

Mile 3.3 Reach your first campsite option. This is a large site on both sides of the trail. Water is from the adjacent creek.

Mile 3.4 Turn left on Panthertown Valley Trail.

Fifteen-foot Frolictown Falls is a block-type waterfall.

Panthertown Waterfalls (cont.)

Mile 3.8 Turn right on Little Green Trail.

Mile 4.0 Reach Schoolhouse Falls, a popular destination due to its large plungepool. You'll want to spend some time here before climbing up and over Little Green Mountain.

Mile 4.5 Reach the top of Little Green Mountain. There are a number of small campsites (but no water), and the trails leading to them may confuse your route. Stick to the main trail leading out to the bare rock slope (and the views), and then bear left along its top edge. If you see a faded white arrow painted on the rock, you're good.

Mile 5.2 Turn left on Macs Gap Trail, heading up the hill.

Mile 5.8 Make a hard right onto Big Green Trail.

Mile 6.6 Turn left on Great Wall Trail. You'll soon descend steps cut in stone leading through a mass of rhododendron.

Mile 7.6 Along the base of the Great Wall, you'll find a couple of good campsites. These are often used by rock climbers. Water is from the adjacent creek.

Mile 7.9 Reach a giant campsite here that also has a huge trail shelter. The shelter alone could easily sleep 20 to 30 people. Water is from the adjacent creek. Just beyond the campsite, Granny Burrell Falls Trail exits to the right. It's 0.3 mile down to the falls. This route continues by fording the creek and turning left.

The plungepool at Schoolhouse Falls is a great place to hang out.

Mile 8.3 Turn left on Deep Gap Trail.

Mile 8.4 Reach Frolictown Falls, a 15-foot cascade. Just beyond it you'll turn right on Wilderness Falls Trail. From here to the falls, the trail is very tight, rooty, and twisty. If you are carrying a wide, tall backpack, you'll have some difficulty. Alternatively, you have the option of returning via Deep Gap Trail.

Mile 8.8 Reach Wilderness Falls. This one is high, close to 80 feet. Be aware that much of the next half-mile is pretty rugged. If you didn't like the last part, you'll hate this. Again, you have to option of returning via Deep Gap Trail.

Mile 9.4 Turn left on Panthertown Valley Trail.

Mile 9.6 Finish.

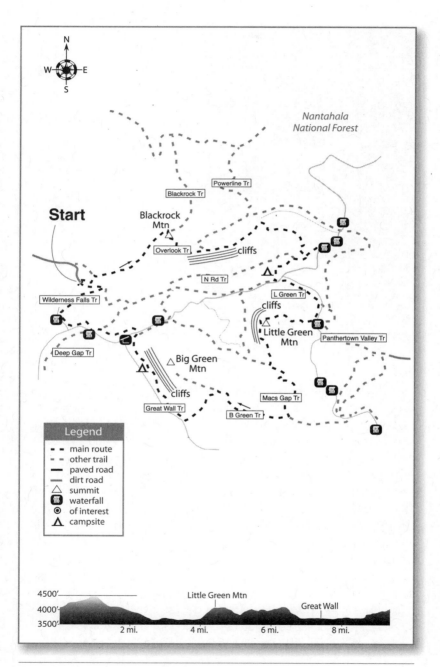

Chattooga Cliffs

Difficulty	Moderate
Hike Distance	5 miles
Type of Hike	Out & Back
Total Ascent	400 ft
Land Manager	USFS
Fee	None

When you reach this bridge, you're near your camping destination.

You'll want to get up pretty early in the morning and get a jump-start on the day to assure yourself a campsite for this trip. There are only two small spots, and one is definitely better than the other. It may be worth the effort to plan your overnight during mid-week and not near a holiday, because the campsite where Whiteside Creek flows into the Chattooga River is an idyllic spot. You'll have everything you need there and more. There's a small waterfall with a deep blue pool at its base. There's a sandy beach. There are big rocks to sun on. There's another, larger pool in the river with a skinny sluice shooting water into it. There's even a footbridge that looks as if it belongs in a fairy land.

The hike itself, though not long, can be technically challenging in places as the trail parallels the Chattooga River. A quick look at the map suggests you'll be hiking along the river the whole way, but the trail climbs high above the river where you catch a glimpse of whitewater only every so often. However, the sound of the Chattooga is a constant companion. High above, on Bull Pen Mountain, are the so-called Chattooga Cliffs.

Getting to the Trailhead

From Highlands, take Main Street east out of town. Soon it becomes Horse Cove Road. After 4.5 miles, turn right on Bull Pen Road and drive another 3.1 miles to Bull Pen Bridge over the Chattooga River. There is a very small parking lot here and a larger one back up the hill you just drove down.

GPS Coordinates

N 35° 00.98′ W 83° 07.60′

Hiking Directions

Begin Walk out the back of the small parking area and onto Chattooga Trail, which follows the river upstream.

Mile 0.6 The little-used Loop Trail exits here on the left.

Mile 0.7 Pass beneath a huge rock overhang.

Mile 1.6 Cross Cane Creek on a steel bridge. Just across the bridge on the left you'll find a very small campsite large enough for one tent. It's not the best

option but will do in a pinch. Water is abundant from Cane Creek. You are well away from the river here.

Mile 1.9 Continue straight as Whiteside Cove Trail enters from the left. You'll get spotty views of the Chattooga Cliffs across the river and high on the sides of Bull Pen Mountain.

Mile 2.5 As you approach the iron bridge over Whiteside Creek, you'll find your campsite for the night. It's none too large, but there is room for a few tents. Just hope no one is there already. Water is abundant from the river or creek, and if it is warm enough you'll find the large pool and sandy beach ideal for swimming. The trail continues along the river for a ways, but there are no more campsites within range. After your night out, turn back from here.

Mile 5.0 Finish.

White violets bloom along the trail in spring.

Chattooga Cliffs Map

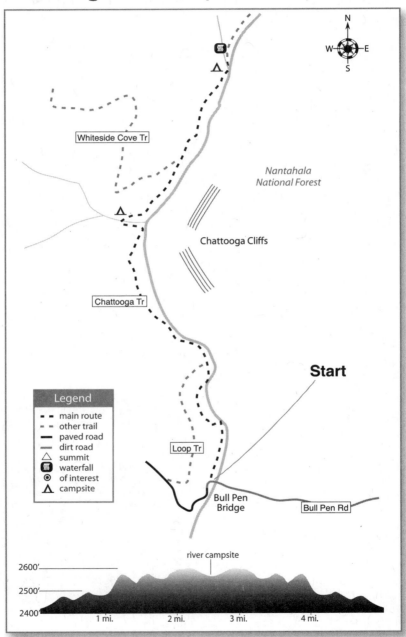

Whiteside Cove Tr

Nantahala National Forest

Chattooga Cliffs

Chattooga Tr

Start

Loop Tr

Bull Pen Bridge

Bull Pen Rd

Legend
- - - main route
- - - other trail
—— paved road
⠿⠿ dirt road
△ summit
🌊 waterfall
⊙ of interest
▲ campsite

river campsite

2600'
2500'
2400'

1 mi.   2 mi.   3 mi.   4 mi.

Whitewater Falls

Difficulty	Easier
Hike Distance	6.6 miles
Type of Hike	Out & Back
Total Ascent	850 ft
Land Manager	USFS
Fee	$2 pc pd

pc=per car pd=per day

This is about as close as you can get to Whitewater Falls.

On this overnight, you'll start the hike in North Carolina, head down into South Carolina on the Foothills Trail to spend the night, then return to North Carolina the next day. It's a way to make a short trip on the long-distance Foothills Trail and see some pretty spectacular waterfalls as you go.

There are actually two Whitewater Falls, upper and lower. Both are very high, and each has a viewing platform for your sightseeing pleasure. One is in North Carolina, and the other is in South Carolina. You'll hike right past the upper falls on the way to your campsite, but to see the lower one you'll need to make a two-mile side trek from the campsite.

Be aware that though this hike is rated easier due to the short distance traveled, climbing back up out of the gorge on day two is nothing close to easy. It's a steep climb. Still, as climbs go, it's not all that long—less than a mile. Just take your time and rest a lot. Also, water is in short supply at the campsite, so fill up before leaving the river corridor, where camping is not allowed.

Whitewater Falls (cont.)

Getting to the Trailhead

From Cashiers, take NC 107 south for 9.4 miles. Just inside South Carolina turn left to follow the sign to Whitewater Falls. Drive 2.2 miles and turn left on SC 130 to drive back into North Carolina where the road becomes NC 281. Go 1.2 miles to the trailhead on the right.

GPS Coordinates

N 35° 01.80' W 83° 00.96'

Hiking Directions

Begin From the info board, walk out the end of the parking area on a paved trail toward the Upper Falls viewing area.

Mile 0.2 Turn right, down the steps (there are a lot of steps) and past the second viewing platform.

Mile 0.4 Junction with Foothills Trail. Turn left and continue descending into the gorge. This trail is quite steep. Watch your footing.

Mile 1.0 Reach the bottom of the gorge where you'll cross the river on an iron bridge.

Mile 2.6 A spur trail to Bad Branch parking area turns right across the river. Turn left to stay on the Foothills Trail.

Mile 3.1 A spur trail turns right, leading to the overlook for Lower Whitewater Falls. Be aware this is a 2-mile round trip with a big elevation change. You may want to check out the overlook after setting up camp for the night. Continue on the Foothills Trail.

Mile 3.2 Reach your campsite for the night. Look for the short trail leading down to it on the right. You'll find that there is room here for 8 or so tents. Water is scarce; look for a seep spring just behind the lower campsite, or go down the short, steep hill to the right of the upper campsite to a tiny stream. After your night out, return the way you came.

Mile 6.4 Finish.

Lower Whitewater Falls as seen from the viewing platform.

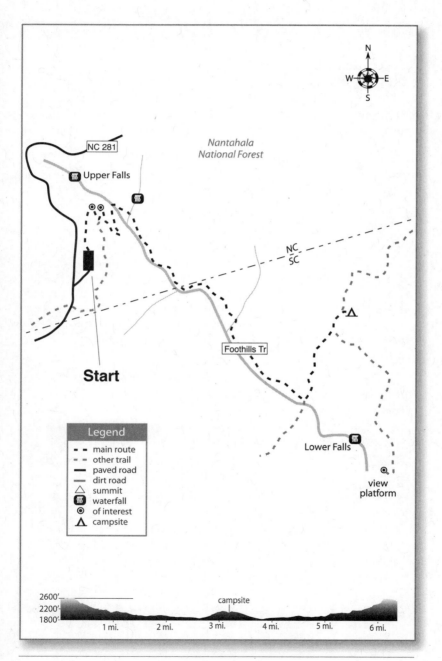

Nantahala National Forest: Highlands Plateau Area   115

Gorges State Park

Contact Information

Gorges State Park
NC 281 South
PO Box 100
Sapphire, NC 28774
828-966-9099
www.ncparks.gov

Permit Required	Yes*
Fee	None
Max Group Size	None
Pets Allowed	On leash

*overnight parking permit

Gorges State Park is one of the newest state parks in North Carolina and still in the development stage. A beautiful visitor center is located in the northwest corner, and you can get the most up-to-date information there or at the ncparks website listed above.

Backpackers have a couple of choices for interesting overnights here. One route leaves the park and heads into Nantahala National Forest, where you can explore the waterfalls along Horsepasture River. For this hike you'll park at a trailhead inside Gorges State Park, where a free parking permit must be filled out at a self-serve station. You just display it on your car windshield. The other hike is much longer and gives you a good tour of the southern section of the state park. Here again, you'll fill out a free parking permit at the trailhead and leave it on your car for the duration of your hike.

Should you be interested, the park does offer a walk-in, fee-based backcountry camping area. A short trail leads down to the campground from the Grassy Ridge Trailhead. You can register for these sites at the same self-serve information kiosk that serves the Horsepasture River waterfalls hike.

Horsepasture Waterfalls

Difficulty	Easier
Hike Distance	4.6 miles
Type of Hike	Out & Back
Total Ascent	1,000 ft
Land Manager	USFS
Fee	None

Rainbow Falls is 125 feet high with a huge plungepool at the bottom.

Most folks hike into the waterfalls along the Horsepasture River for a day excursion. During the summer, it's a great place to picnic, swim, and generally cool off in the water. Sliding into the plungepool over the lip of Turtleback Falls is, for some, a rite of passage. Imagine, then, spending the night down near the river where, after most of the daytrippers go home, you can have a little more solitude. That's what you can do on this overnight.

Your access point for this route is Gorges State Park. Here you'll find a large trailhead parking area that accommodates the many day users as well as the overnight campers who are walking into the developed overnight-use area of the park. Even though you're hiking into the National Forest from here, this lot is for you. The trail quickly leads down to the river where there are a few choices for campsites. Though not as developed as those in the park (no tent pads or lantern hooks), they have the advantage of being next to the river. Once you've set up camp, the river and falls are there to enjoy until you decide to hike out the next day.

Horsepasture Waterfalls (cont.)

Getting to the Trailhead

From Brevard, drive 18.5 miles west on US 64. In Sapphire, turn left on NC 281. Drive 1.0 mile to Gorges State Park and continue past the visitor center 1.8 miles to the Grassy Ridge Trailhead parking lot.

Note: You must register to park your car overnight. Do so at the trailhead information board; it's free.

GPS Coordinates
N 35° 05.33' W 82° 57.12'

Hiking Directions

Begin Walk out the trail blazed with blue and orange dots.

Mile 0.3 Turn right on Rainbow Falls Trail.

Mile 0.8 Enter the Nantahala National Forest.

Mile 1.0 An unmarked trail turns off here and leads steeply down to Stairstep Falls. There is also a small, isolated campsite at the bottom on the trail near the falls. You may consider this as a

camping destination; otherwise continue on Rainbow Falls Trail.

Mile 1.1 At this stream crossing you'll find a large campsite with several options for tents along the small stream and more down by the river. It's the best choice of sites along the Horsepasture. Water is from the creek or the river. If you camp here you can continue to the various waterfalls without your pack.

Mile 1.6 Reach Rainbow Falls.

Mile 2.0 Reach Turtleback Falls.

Mile 2.1 You'll find another campsite option here. It's small, and realize you'll be camping just below NC 281.

Mile 2.3 End of the trail with a view of Drift Falls, which is on private property. Return to the start from this point.

Mile 4.6 Finish.

Turtleback Falls is a favorite destination for water lovers in summer.

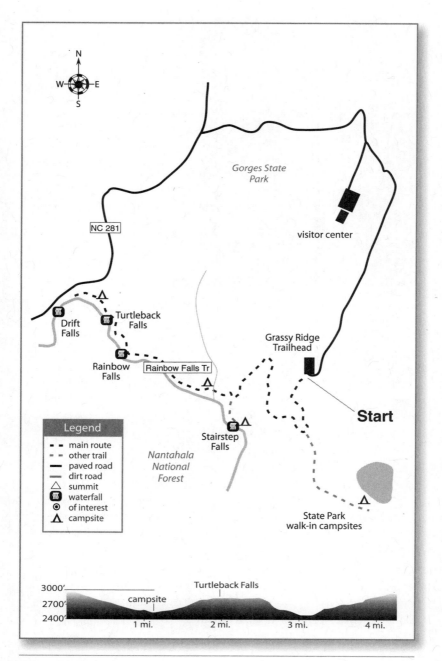

Gorges Loop

Difficulty	Strenuous
Hike Distance	19.1 miles
Type of Hike	Loop
Total Ascent	3,900 ft
Land Manager	State Park
Fee	None*

* Overnight parking Pass Required

You'll cross the Toxaway River on this bouncy Foothills Trail suspension bridge.

Much of the 77-mile Foothills Trail is in South Carolina, but there is a section that travels through North Carolina. On this hike you'll walk along it for about six miles as it makes its way through the lower regions of Gorges State Park, one of the newest state parks in North Carolina. Since this park is so new, most of the trails are old roads, so the tread is wide and easy to maintain for hikers. This park has only two backcountry campsites, and one of them is located along this route.

You'll leave the park's Frozen Creek Road trailhead on Canebrake Trail, heading down to Lake Jocassee and the Foothills Trail. It's a nice downhill walk, and you'll find a delightful campsite on the lake. Once you cross the footbridge over the Toxaway River, expect the easy walking to come to an abrupt end as the route climbs up and down; some of the ups can get pretty darn steep. You'll find a second campsite option by taking a half-mile detour from the park. After that it's more climbing and two deep stream crossings before finishing the hike.

Getting to the Trailhead

From the junction of US 64 and NC 215 west of Rosman, travel 1.0 mile and turn left on Frozen Creek Road. Continue another 3.1 miles to the Frozen Creek Trailhead on the right.

GPS Coordinates
N 35° 06.51' W 82° 53.03'

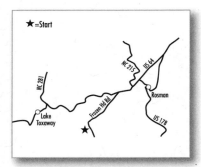

Hiking Directions

Begin Follow Auger Hole/Canebrake Trail out of the parking lot behind the information kiosk.

Mile 0.8 Turn left on Canebrake Trail (yellow blazes) and soon begin a long descent to the Toxaway River and Lake Jocassee.

Mile 4.7 Bear right as a road enters from the left.

Mile 5.3 Reach Foothills Trail junction. If you plan to spend the night here, reach the campsites by turning left across the bridge. You'll find three large sites right on the river/lake. There are tables, fire rings, and even lantern hangers. The route continues by turning right on Foothills Trail and crossing

the Toxaway River on a high suspension bridge. Over the next five miles you'll follow the lake shore and then climb very steeply in places as the trail traverses the lower reaches of the park.

Mile 10.5 Reach the park boundary below a set of high-voltage powerlines. The route continues by turning right on Auger Hole Trail. However, if you want a campsite closer to the midpoint of the hike, continue straight on Foothills Trail.

Mile 11.2 Here you'll find a small but pleasant campsite on Bear Creek in a grove of white pines. It's a nice spot. After a night out here, retrace your steps to the park boundary and turn left up the very steep hill under the powerlines on Auger Hole Trail.

Mile 13.3 Reach Turkeypen Gap. Go around the gate and turn right to continue on Auger Hole Trail.

Mile 14.3 Make a wet stream crossing. Just upstream is a small waterfall.

Mile 15.4 Make another wet stream crossing, this time crossing the Toxaway River.

Mile 18.3 Turn left as you close the loop to continue on the combined Auger Hole and Canebrake Trails.

Mile 19.1 Finish.

Gorges Loop Map

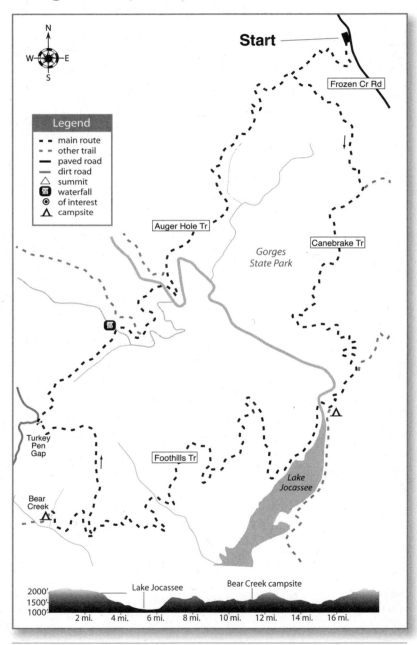

BACKPACKING OVERNIGHTS—NC MOUNTAINS / SC UPSTATE

Pisgah National Forest

Contact Information

Appalachian Ranger District
PO Box 128
Burnsville, NC 28714
828-682-6146
www.fs.usda.gov/nfsnc
(hikes pp. 125-127)

Pisgah Ranger District
1600 Pisgah Hwy
Pisgah Forest, NC 28768
828-877-3265
www.fs.usda.gov/nfsnc
(hikes pp. 128-159)

Grandfather Ranger District
109 E Lawing Dr
Nebo, NC 28761
828-652-2144
www.fs.usda.gov/nfsnc
(hikes pp. 160-166)

Permit Required	No*
Fee	None
Max Group Size	See below
Pets Allowed	Yes

*see below for Linville Gorge

Pisgah National Forest covers over 500,000 acres from the North Carolina high country near Virginia, down the spine of the Appalachians bordering Tennessee, and south to the Pisgah District. It's the birthplace of modern forestry, straddling the Blue Ridge Parkway west of Asheville. It's also rugged territory with the highest mountains east of the Mississippi within its borders—many over 6,000 feet. Pisgah is divided into three districts.

In the **Appalachian Ranger District** north of Asheville, most overnight backpacking opportunities occur along the Appalachian National Scenic Trail; your best bet is to hike out to a specific destination, then on your return the next day, retrace your steps. One of the most scenic routes described in this book is at Max Patch, a popular high bald north of Waynesville (p. 125). Another option is to use two vehicles or arrange a shuttle and hike a point-to-point route along the Appalachian Trail. Sections of two other hikes listed in this book are in the Appalachian District. On both Commissary Ridge (p. 168) and Crest of the Blacks (p. 171) you'll spend the night in the National Forest, beginning and ending the hike in Mt. Mitchell State Park, where state park rules apply (see p. 167).

Pisgah District is by far the most popular destination for overnight hiking. With hundreds of miles of trail to choose from, it's no wonder. You'll hike past waterfalls, through wilderness areas, and over 6,000-foot peaks. As rugged as it is, there are still relatively easy routes to choose from—great for beginners or those with a limited amount of time. No permits are required anywhere in the district, and you'll find plenty of campsites on most any hike you choose. Of course you'll want to use good Leave No Trace skills (see p. 24) and always choose an established campsite with an established fire ring to minimize the impact to this treasured resource.

Several hikes in this guide travel through the Shining Rock Wilderness Area (pp. 147-162), where rules stipulate a group size limit of 10 and open fires are not permitted. This means no campfires, even though you'll likely see that those before you have broken this rule. Devastating wildfires are in part responsible for the open expanses you'll see in the higher elevations of Shining Rock. More fire up here would not be good.

In the **Grandfather District** you'll find the bulk of trails suitable for overnight backpacking trips are either in Linville Gorge Wilderness or the Wilson Creek area. In both, the trails can be pretty tough and are less well maintained—often going straight uphill instead of using switchbacks. Bridges over rivers and streams are also few and far between. That said, Linville Gorge is a spectacular place for overnight hiking. It's also a popular place. For this reason, permits are required for overnights in the Gorge on all weekends and holidays from May 1 to October 31. The permit is good for a two-night/three-day maximum stay, with a limit of one permit per month. You can get a permit by mail or in person from the Grandfather Ranger District office in Nebo, or in person from the Gorge Info Cabin located 0.4 mile from NC 183 on Kistler Memorial Highway (a dirt road) near Linville Falls. Only 50 permits are issued per weekend/holiday. For overnight stays during the week or between October 31 and May 1, no permit is required.

Max Patch Shelter

Difficulty	Easier
Hike Distance	5 miles
Type of Hike	Out & Back
Total Ascent	850 ft
Land Manager	USFS
Fee	None

This log cabin-style shelter is your destination for a night out on the Appalachian Trail.

Max Patch is a happening place. Even on a sunny Sunday in midwinter, you'll find the trailhead parking lot full. Expect to see dog walkers, kite flyers, and people just hanging out. What makes this place so attractive? It's one of the few balds in the southern Appalachians that you can drive right up to. Hop out of your car and immediately you're hiking in wide open fields with less than a half-mile to the summit. The views are spectacular. The great thing about this hike is that most all of the hordes of people head back to where they came from before the sun goes down. They're just here for the day; you're here for the night.

On day one, you'll circle the base of Max Patch and then hop on the Appalachian Trail for the climb up and over the top. Take your time on this stretch and enjoy the view. Once over the top, you'll stay on the AT all the way out to Roaring Fork Shelter, a log cabin-style shelter with three sides and an open front. There's room for six to eight folks on the flat platform in the shelter and more room for tents nearby. On day two you'll return to Max Patch, where you can lunch on top before returning to the trailhead.

Max Patch Shelter (cont.)

Getting to the Trailhead

From exit 7 on I-40 near the Tennessee line, take Cold Spring Road east for 6.3 miles. Turn hard left onto SR 1182 and continue 2.0 miles to the Max Patch Trailhead.

GPS Coordinates
N 35° 47.78' W 82° 57.76'

Hiking Directions

Begin Walk out the back of the parking lot and bear right around the base of Max Patch. You'll see evidence that some people head straight up the mountain here, which is frowned upon.

Mile 0.4 Turn left on the Appalachian Trail to climb up and over Max Patch Mountain.

Mile 0.9 Reach the summit of Max Patch. Enjoy the views, then continue over the top on the AT.

Mile 1.0 Continue straight on the AT as the loop trail turns off to the left.

Mile 1.5 Continue on the AT as a trail enters from the right.

Mile 1.7 Reach a small campsite where the AT loops past a fence. This is a good option if you don't want to go all the way to the shelter. Water is from a nearby spring.

Mile 1.8 Buckeye Ridge Trail enters from the right; go left to continue on the AT.

Mile 1.9 Go left to continue on the AT as Buckeye Ridge Trail exits on the right.

Mile 2.5 A side trail leads 20 feet to a stream that is the water source for the shelter just ahead.

Mile 2.7 Turn right on a side trail leading to the shelter. You can see it from here. There are several tent spots just beyond if the shelter itself is full. After your night out, return to Max Patch the way you came.

Mile 4.5 Turn right here to bypass the summit.

Mile 5.0 Finish.

Posts mark the route of the Appalachian Trail.

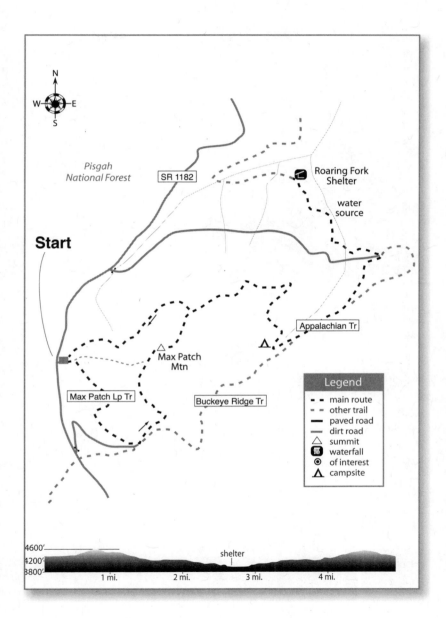

John Rock

Difficulty	Easier
Hike Distance	5.8 miles
Type of Hike	Loop
Total Ascent	1,000 ft
Land Manager	USFS
Fee	None

You'll get a wide open view from the top of John Rock.

There are no shortage of camping spots to choose from on this overnight trip. It's a good thing, as this is a very popular area. One look at the view from the trailhead and you can see why folks flock here. To the north is Looking Glass Rock, its dome like a giant gray turtle poking up into the air. To the immediate south and just above you is John Rock, another cliff-faced dome. Back behind you is Cedar Rock with its curtain-shaped cliffs. Many folks come for the day to explore the Pisgah Fish Hatchery and the Center For Wildlife Education. Others are here to fish in the Davidson River, perhaps secretly hoping all the hatchery fish will make a sudden mass escape over the fence.

Your biggest decision will be whether to set up camp before your hike over John Rock or after. Either way, you should easily find a spot to suit your needs. All are situated near small streams where water is abundant, and one is right beside a small waterfall.

Getting to the Trailhead

From the Pisgah District Ranger Station just north of the town of Pisgah Forest on US 276, drive north 3.7 miles. Turn left toward the Pisgah Fish Hatchery and Wildlife Education Center and drive 1.5 miles. The trailhead is at the Fish Hatchery.

GPS Coordinates
N 35° 17.07' W 82° 47.47'

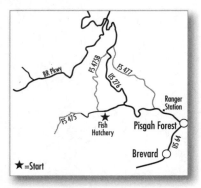

Hiking Directions

Begin Walk past the entrance to the wildlife center and around the gate, then turn right on Cat Gap Loop Trail (orange blaze).

Mile 0.3 Cross a footbridge and then cross a small dirt road.

Mile 0.7 Listen and look. You first should hear the waterfall and then see an unmarked trail leading down to it. It's a nice side trip before continuing on the route.

Mile 0.9 Down beside the creek at the base of a small waterfall is a nice campsite with room for 2

or 3 small tents. Water is from the adjacent creek.

Mile 1.0 Junction with Butter Gap Trail. Here are a few more campsite options, both just before the junction and across the creek. Turn left here and cross the creek to remain on Cat Gap Loop Trail.

Mile 1.3 Reach a large campsite in a white pine grove. Water is from the adjacent creek.

Mile 1.5 Reach another campsite in a white pine grove and yet another across the stream. Water is from the creek.

Mile 1.6 This is the last campsite before the climb. Water is from the adjacent small creek.

Mile 2.0 Turn left on Cat Gap Bypass Trail (yellow blaze).

Mile 2.7 Reach a gap and trail junction. Turn left here on John Rock Trail, following yellow blaze.

Mile 2.8 A short huffer-puffer climb brings you to the first summit of John Rock.

Mile 3.5 Just after passing through a dry campsite you'll reach John Rock itself, where the views are just awesome. Stay clear of the edge!

Mile 4.4 Turn left, back onto Cat Gap Loop Trail.

Mile 4.5 Reach the first of several campsites between here and the trailhead. All have the same stream for a water source.

Mile 5.8 Finish.

John Rock Map

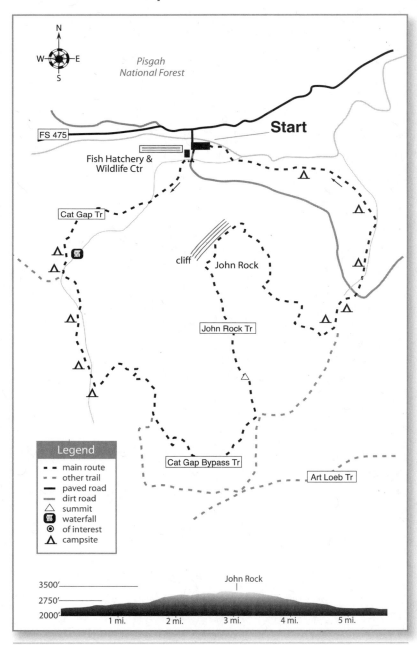

Pisgah National Forest

FS 475

Start

Fish Hatchery & Wildlife Ctr

Cat Gap Tr

cliff

John Rock

John Rock Tr

Cat Gap Bypass Tr

Art Loeb Tr

Legend

- - - main route
- - - other trail
— paved road
— dirt road
△ summit
♨ waterfall
◉ of interest
▲ campsite

3500'
2750'
2000'

John Rock

1 mi. 2 mi. 3 mi. 4 mi. 5 mi.

Butter Gap

Butter Gap shelter looks like a giant wooden tent and functions as one.

Difficulty	Moderate
Hike Distance	8.3 miles
Type of Hike	Loop
Total Ascent	1,600 ft
Land Manager	USFS
Fee	None

There are only three overnight shelters in the Pisgah District, and on this hike you'll have the opportunity to stay in one. Here's what you need to know about camping out in a shelter: In inclement weather, they are the best. There's no need set up a tent (or take down a wet one) in the rain—you just walk right up and call it home. Plus, they actually reduce the amount of wear and tear on the forest. Sure, the area around them can be beaten down, but tent sites tend to get worn down even more with folks constantly clearing out different spots. Those are some of the good qualities of a shelter. On the down side, they are often crowded and can attract rodents and other critters. And don't assume the shelter will be available. Always bring a tent or tarp, just in case.

The great thing about this route is that there are lots of campsites to choose from all along the way. If you get a late start you'll find campsites early on, and if you planned to use the shelter but it turned out to be full, there are more campsites beyond it. Highlights include two pretty water-falls and the looming cliffs of Cedar Rock Mountain.

Butter Gap (cont.)

Getting to the Trailhead

From the Pisgah District Ranger Station just north of the town of Pisgah Forest on US 276, drive north 3.7 miles. Turn left toward the Pisgah Fish Hatchery and Wildlife Education Center and drive 1.5 miles. The trailhead is at the Fish Hatchery.

GPS Coordinates
N 35° 17.07' W 82° 47.47'

★ =Start

Hiking Directions

Begin Walk past the entrance to the wildlife center and around the gate, then turn right on Cat Gap Loop Trail (orange blazes).

Mile 0.3 Cross a footbridge and then a small dirt road.

Mile 0.7 Pass a waterfall down a short side trail on the left.

Mile 0.9 Down beside the creek and at the base of a small waterfall is a nice campsite with room for 2 or 3 small tents. Water is from the adjacent creek.

Mile 1.0 Junction with Butter Gap Trail. Here are a few more campsite options, just before the junction and in the field after the turn. Turn right on Butter Gap Trail.

Mile 1.4 Long Branch Trail exits right. Stay on Butter Gap Trail.

Mile 1.9 Pass a waterfall down a short side trail on the left.

Mile 2.0 There is small campsite here on the creek.

Mile 2.7 Pass a campsite on the left and then a large campsite on the right. Water is from the creek.

Mile 3.6 Reach Butter Gap. Many trails converge here. Go straight onto the Art Loeb Trail.

Mile 3.7 Reach Butter Gap Shelter. The water source is a small stream crossing the trail a bit farther on.

Mile 4.7 Pass a small campsite. There is water farther up the trail.

Mile 5.1 Reach a gap with a campsite at the base of Cedar Rock, a good place for bouldering. Water is from a small creek.

Mile 6.1 Reach Cat Gap. Continue straight across onto Cat Gap Trail.

Mile 6.4 Reach Horse Cove Gap. Turn right to stay on Cat Gap Trail. You'll pass several more campsites on your way back to the trailhead.

Mile 6.9 John Rock Trail enters from the left.

Mile 8.3 Finish.

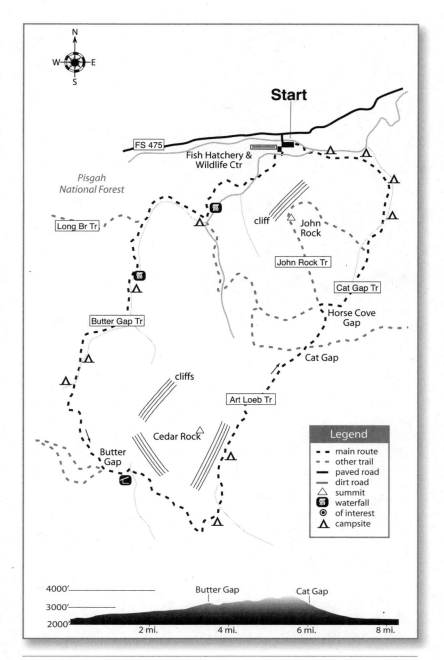

Start

FS 475

Fish Hatchery &
Wildlife Ctr

Pisgah
National Forest

Long Br Tr

cliff

John
Rock

John Rock Tr

Cat Gap Tr

Horse Cove
Gap

Butter Gap Tr

Cat Gap

cliffs

Art Loeb Tr

Cedar Rock

Butter
Gap

Legend

- - - main route
- - - other trail
——— paved road
——— dirt road
△ summit
♨ waterfall
◉ of interest
⛺ campsite

4000'
3000'
2000'

Butter Gap

Cat Gap

2 mi.   4 mi.   6 mi.   8 mi.

Pisgah National Forest: Pisgah District

Deep Gap

Farlow Gap Trail crosses several streams with waterfalls.

Difficulty	Strenuous
Hike Distance	18.7 miles
Type of Hike	Loop
Total Ascent	4,500 ft
Land Manager	USFS
Fee	None

Deep Gap is seriously deep in the backcountry, and no matter how you slice it, it's a long walk to get there. Something can be said for hiking into such a remote location. It's the kind of place where, when you arrive, you feel a real sense of accomplishment. This is something to keep in mind when you're huffing and puffing and sweating and guzzling water as you scale the steep trail to Farlow Gap. Give yourself plenty of time to get up this one.

You'll walk a long way on this hike, and you could easily spread it out by adding another day. If you can swing it, plan a night at Deep Gap. Stay in the trail shelter located right on the Art Loeb Trail or at one of the several campsites on the nearby old woods road. Either is a good choice, and if it's the heat of summer you can take advantage of nature's air conditioning (it's cool up here) and get a reprieve from the heat. The route passes several waterfalls and goes right over the top of Pilot Mountain, where the views are grand. Feeling energetic? Get an early start on day two and catch the sunrise from the top of Pilot Mountain.

Getting to the Trailhead

From the Pisgah District Ranger Station just north of the town of Pisgah Forest on US 276, drive north 3.7 miles. Turn left toward Pisgah Fish Hatchery and Wildlife Education Center and drive 1.5 miles. The trailhead is at the Fish Hatchery.

GPS Coordinates
N 35° 17.07′ W 82° 47.47′

★=Start

Hiking Directions

Begin Walk out the entrance to the fish hatchery and turn left on FS 475.

Mile 0.6 Turn left off the road onto Davidson River Trail.

Mile 1.9 Turn right on FS 475 and then left into the entrance to Cove Creek Group Camp.

Mile 2.3 Turn left on Caney Bottom Trail just before entering the group camp.

Mile 2.4 Caney Bottom Trail turns right here and crosses a small creek. Stay straight on an unmarked trail leading uphill.

Mile 2.6 Turn left here on the grassy FS 5046.

Mile 2.8 Pass a high waterfall on the right.

Mile 2.9 You should see a big bridge ahead and several walk-in roadside camping spots along the Davidson River. Turn right before reaching the bridge on Daniel Ridge Trail.

Mile 3.9 Down a steep side trail is a nice campsite just below a waterfall and swimming hole. This is a good option if you're spreading this hike over more than one night.

Mile 4.1 The trail turns to the right here at an old bridge site and then begins to climb in earnest.

Mile 4.7 Turn left on Farlow Gap Trail.

Mile 7.0 Cross the top of a waterfall. This is a good spot to take a break. Ahead lies a very steep 1-mile climb.

Mile 7.6 Right here in the middle of the steep stuff is a small campsite with a little creek nearby. You could stay here, but it's good to get the worst part of the climb behind you.

Mile 8.0 Reach Farlow Gap. Here you have choice to make. You can turn left on Art Loeb Trail and climb up and over Sassafras Knob to the Deep Gap Shelter, or you can turn left on the old roadbed that takes you to the same place without climbing. Art

Deep Gap (cont.)

Loeb Trail takes you directly to the shelter. Turn back to the right at Deep Gap after crossing the small stream to get there. You'll also see several good campsites along the old road if you prefer not to use the shelter. Water is from the small stream at Deep Gap. From Deep Gap, the route continues on the Art Loeb Trail.

Mile 9.7 Summit Pilot Mountain and enjoy the views in all directions from here. Tune your ear to the west and you might hear Courthouse Falls thundering below. Continue to follow Art Loeb Trail down the mountain. You'll cross FS 229 twice.

Mile 11.7 Reach Gloucester Gap. Cross the road to continue on Art Loeb Trail.

Mile 12.3 Cross FS 471.

Mile 14.9 Turn left on Butter Gap Trail at this trails junction.

Mile 15.1 Reach Butter Gap. Turn left to continue down Butter Gap Trail.

Mile 15.8 You'll see a nice campsite on the left here. Water is from an adjacent stream.

Mile 16.0 Another good campsite is located here with water from the creek.

Mile 16.1 Pass a waterfall on the right.

Mile 16.5 Long Branch Trail exits left. Stay on Butter Gap Trail.

Mile 17.0 Reach Picklesimer Fields. Turn left on Cat Gap Trail. You'll follow it all the way back to the trailhead.

Mile 18.7 Finish.

Early morning fog lingers in the valleys below Pilot Mountain.

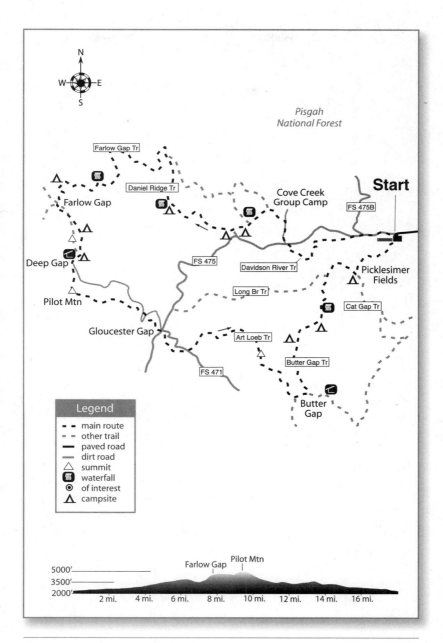

Start

Pisgah
National Forest

Farlow Gap Tr

Daniel Ridge Tr

Cove Creek
Group Camp

FS 475B

Farlow Gap

Deep Gap

Pilot Mtn

Gloucester Gap

FS 475

Davidson River Tr

Long Br Tr

Picklesimer
Fields

Cat Gap Tr

Art Loeb Tr

Butter Gap Tr

FS 471

Butter
Gap

Legend

- – – main route
- - - - other trail
- —— paved road
- —— dirt road
- △ summit
- 🌊 waterfall
- ⊙ of interest
- ▲ campsite

5000'
3500'
2000'

Farlow Gap

Pilot Mtn

2 mi. 4 mi. 6 mi. 8 mi. 10 mi. 12 mi. 14 mi. 16 mi.

Caney Bottom

Difficulty	Easier
Hike Distance	4.9 miles
Type of Hike	Loop
Total Ascent	650 ft
Land Manager	USFS
Fee	None

Take the time for a slide on Baby Sliding Rock early in the trip.

If you are looking for a great first-time out overnight in the Pisgah area, this is it. You'll see several waterfalls, hike what feels like relatively level terrain, spend the night in a big shady campsite, and not cover too many miles. One highlight of the hike is Baby Sliding Rock. You can slide down this small waterfall just like on its larger namesake on Looking Glass Creek farther to the north. There will be far fewer people, and the action is a bit tamer. So if it's warm out, give yourself time for a slide.

The first day you'll walk through dense foliage as the trail twists and turns alongside Caney Bottom Creek. When you reach Cove Creek Trail, you've reached your home for the night. There's plenty of room to spread out in this big, level campsite. On day two, the route takes you a bit farther up and then works its way slowly down. Along the way you'll pass Cove Creek Falls. This is a high one, and there's a side trail that leads down to the bottom for a good view back up. Take care to not get near the edge.

Best of all, if you're into jumping into icy water, there's a small waterfall and swimming hole right at the trailhead called Whaleback. Check it out.

Getting to the Trailhead

From the Pisgah District Ranger Station just north of the town of Pisgah Forest on US 276, drive north 3.7 miles. Turn left toward the Pisgah Fish Hatchery and Wildlife Education Center and continue 4.7 miles on FS 475 to the entrance to Cove Creek Group Camp. The trailhead is on the left.

GPS Coordinates
N 35° 16.98′ W 82° 49.02′

★ =Start

Hiking Directions

Begin Walk across the road and around the gate on the entrance road into Cove Creek Group Camp. Look for a footbridge to the right of the stream ford.

Mile 0.4 Caney Bottom Trail enters from the left. Stay on the road as you walk through the group camp.

Mile 0.5 Just beyond the first open field of the group camp,

look to the right for Baby Sliding Rock, a big waterslide.

Mile 0.7 Continue across the second open field and onto the foot trail beyond.

Mile 0.9 Follow the Caney Bottom Trail (blue blaze) that bypassed the campground.

Mile 1.9 Reach a 4-way trail junction. The route turns left here, but go right to immediately find the best campsite on the loop. Water is from the stream you'll cross on the route when you go left on Cove Creek Trail (yellow blaze). This is a large campsite.

Mile 2.2 Continuing on the loop, you'll find a second campsite here on the right. Water is from a small stream nearby.

Mile 2.6 At a creek crossing, you'll find a small campsite right on the trail.

Mile 3.6 A side trail here leads to Cove Creek Falls. Leave your packs here, as the trail is steep down to the view spot.

Mile 4.1 Cove Creek Trail ends here. Continue straight onto Caney Bottom Trail. The group campground is now down to your left.

Mile 4.4 Cross a small stream and turn left to stay on Caney Bottom Trail.

Mile 4.5 Turn right on the entrance road to close the loop.

Mile 4.9 Finish.

Caney Bottom Map

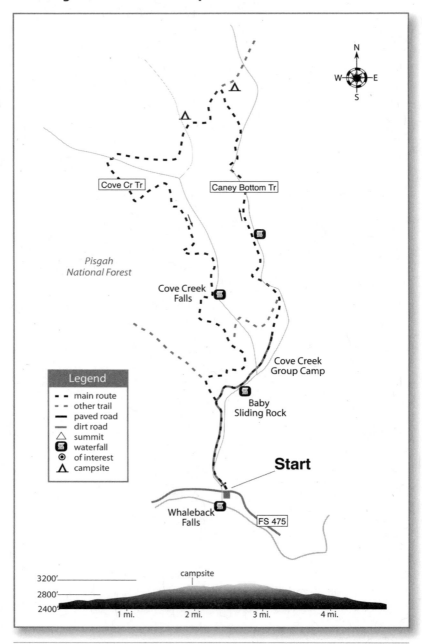

Legend

- – – main route
- – – other trail
- — paved road
- — dirt road
- △ summit
- 🌊 waterfall
- ⊙ of interest
- ▲ campsite

Cove Cr Tr

Caney Bottom Tr

Pisgah
National Forest

Cove Creek
Falls

Cove Creek
Group Camp

Baby
Sliding Rock

Start

Whaleback
Falls

FS 475

N
W — E
S

campsite

3200'
2800'
2400'

1 mi.   2 mi.   3 mi.   4 mi.

Clawhammer Mountain

Difficulty	Moderate
Hike Distance	13.3 miles
Type of Hike	Loop
Total Ascent	4,050 ft
Land Manager	USFS
Fee	None

The views of Looking Glass Rock are pretty good from the cliffs atop Clawhammer.

There's a fair amount of climbing on this route, but it's rated moderate since the hills are spread out pretty evenly. Just when you get tired of going up, you get a reprieve and go down. It's also a good year-round route. You start right on US 276 at the Coontree Picnic Area, just up from the ranger station. The elevations are not so high that roads are closed or trails become impassable due to winter conditions. During the warmer months the wildflowers are awesome, and if there is time, you can cool off at the end of your hike in the swimming hole beside the picnic area. *And* your overnight stay is at a trail shelter where you can stay dry, no matter what the weather is doing.

From the picnic area, you immediately begin to climb up Coontree Mountain. Once on top you'll begin a long ridgewalk where every so often you'll dip down to a gap. At times the ridges seem razor thin with steep drop-offs on both sides. You'll gain more altitude with each successive mountain until finally on day two you'll crest Clawhammer Mountain, from which there is an impressive clifftop view.

Clawhammer Mountain (cont.)

Getting to the Trailhead

From the Pisgah Ranger Station drive north on US 276 for 3.3 miles. The trailhead is at Coontree Picnic Area on the left.

GPS Coordinates

N 35° 17.36' W 82° 45.81'

★ =Start

Hiking Directions

Begin Walk across the highway and onto the Coontree Loop Trail.

Mile 0.2 Take the left fork of the loop trail and head up the mountain for your first steep climb.

Mile 1.8 Turn left on Bennett Gap Trail.

Mile 2.3 Perry Cove Trail exits downhill to the right.

Mile 2.5 Reach a great view spot for Looking Glass Rock.

Mile 3.2 Cross FS 477 at Bennett Gap onto Buckwheat Knob Trail. There are a couple of steep uphills ahead.

Mile 4.7 Reach Club Gap. Continue straight up the hill on Black Mountain Trail.

Mile 5.5 Barnett Branch Trail exits left. Stay straight.

Mile 6.5 Reach Buckhorn Gap Shelter and campsite, your accommodation for the evening. This is the only campsite on this route. Water is from a good spring behind the shelter, which sleeps 6 on wooden bunks. There's room for tents out front.

Mile 6.7 Go down steps to Buckhorn Gap. Black Mountain Trail continues across FS 5058. Begin your ascent of Clawhammer Mountain.

Mile 7.9 Top out finally on Clawhammer, where you'll find a nice clifftop view looking west over Pisgah.

Mile 9.5 Turn right on FS 5022 at Pressley Gap.

Mile 9.7 Look closely for a set of wooden steps heading left off the road. Turn left down these on Pressley Cove Trail.

Mile 10.9 At the bottom of the hill you'll reach FS 477. Turn left, cross the bridge, and then turn right on Bennett Gap Trail to begin your final climb.

Mile 12.0 Turn left on Coontree Loop Trail.

Mile 13.0 Reach the other end of Coontree Loop Trail. Continue straight back to the trailhead.

Mile 13.3 Finish.

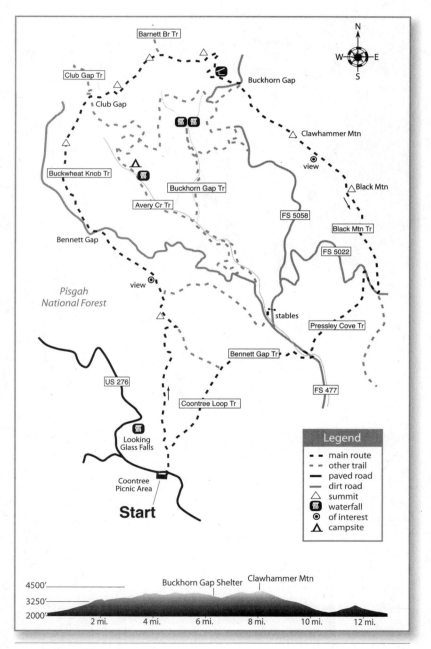

Buckhorn Gap

Difficulty	Moderate
Hike Distance	9.4 miles
Type of Hike	Loop
Total Ascent	2,000 ft
Land Manager	USFS
Fee	None

Two waterfalls are side by side at Twin Falls, which you'll see on day two.

On this excursion, you'll hike up to the Buckhorn Gap shelter for your night out in the woods. This shelter is different than the other two in the Pisgah District—it has bunks and sleeps six people. Obviously these are not your standard dorm bunks with mattresses, but individual wooden platforms on which to lay your own camp pad. Out in front of the shelter is a nice fire pit, on the side is a wide shelf to cook on, and just around back is a bubbling spring where you can get your water as it comes up out of the ground. It doesn't get any purer.

The hike starts with a climb up alongside Avery Creek, past a secluded waterfall, and finally up to Club Gap. The climbing does not end here as you still have to climb up and over the razorback spine of Rich Mountain before tramping down to the shelter. Then your climbing is over for this trip.

Day two takes you down to Buckhorn Gap and then on down to Twin Falls, a double waterfall and a good place to break for a snack or lunch before finishing the hike.

Getting to the Trailhead

From the Pisgah District Ranger Station just north of the town of Pisgah Forest on US 276, drive north 0.5 mile and turn right on FS 477. Continue another 2.3 miles to the Buckhorn Gap trailhead on the right.

GPS Coordinates
N 35° 18.97' W 82° 45.13'

★=Start

Hiking Directions

Begin Walk down Buckhorn Gap Trail (orange blaze).

Mile 0.9 Just before the creek, bear left on Avery Creek/Buckhorn Gap Trail.

Mile 1.0 Turn left on Avery Creek Trail (blue blaze). Buckhorn Gap Trail heads right across the creek on a footbridge.

Mile 1.8 Pass a large but seldom used campsite on the right. Water is from the adjacent stream.

Mile 2.4 Continue straight across an old road.

Mile 3.3 Reach Club Gap. Turn right on Black Mountain Trail (white blaze).

Mile 4.2 Barnett Branch Trail exits left. Continue straight on.

Mile 5.2 Reach Buckhorn Gap Shelter, which has bunks for 6 people and room for tents out front. Water is from a good spring behind the shelter. Other than the campsite you passed earlier, this is your only option for camping on this loop. Continue on down the trail after your night out.

Mile 5.4 Go down steps to Buckhorn Gap, cross the road on the Black Mountain Trail, and then take a right just as you enter the woods on Buckhorn Gap Trail (orange blaze).

Mile 5.8 Turn left on FS 5058.

Mile 6.3 Turn right, back onto Buckhorn Gap Trail.

Mile 6.6 Turn right to continue on Buckhorn Gap Trail.

Mile 7.1 Turn right to hike up and view Twin Falls.

Mile 7.3 Reach Twin Falls. Have a look and then return to Buckhorn Gap Trail to continue.

Mile 8.4 You've been here before. Close the loop and continue back to the trailhead the way you came in.

Mile 9.4 Finish.

Buckhorn Gap Map

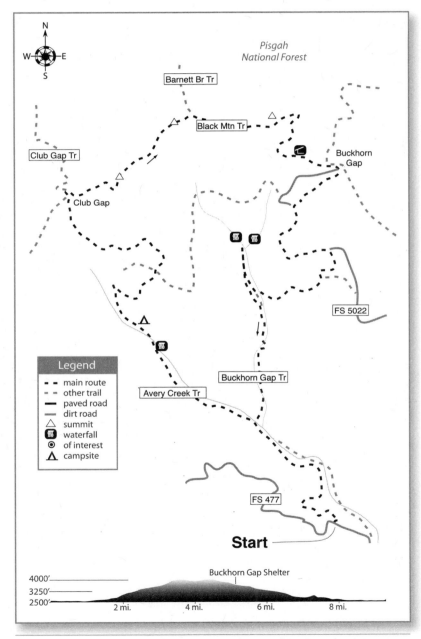

Pisgah National Forest

Barnett Br Tr

Black Mtn Tr

Club Gap Tr

Buckhorn Gap

Club Gap

FS 5022

Buckhorn Gap Tr

Avery Creek Tr

Legend
- - - main route
- - - other trail
— paved road
— dirt road
△ summit
🌊 waterfall
◉ of interest
⛰ campsite

FS 477

Start

Buckhorn Gap Shelter

4000'
3250'
2500'
2 mi.   4 mi.   6 mi.   8 mi.

Big East Fork

In the higher elevations the trail tunnels through the trees.

Difficulty	Strenuous
Hike Distance	12.7 miles
Type of Hike	Loop
Total Ascent	3,000 ft
Land Manager	USFS
Fee	None

Get ready for a pretty rugged overnight hike. Most people get into the upper regions of the Shining Rock Wilderness by starting from the Black Balsam trailhead, just off the Blue Ridge Parkway. On this route, you'll start much lower and climb 3,000 feet in just over four miles. A 700-foot-per-mile gain translates into pretty darn steep and is one of the main reasons this hike is rated strenuous. The fact that you're in a wilderness area with exposed terrain, river and stream crossings, and mostly unmarked trails is the other reason.

This is one of those routes where the sheer beauty of the woods is equal to the panoramic views. You'll walk through fern-filled glades, exquisite wildflower displays, and places where brilliant green grass grows lush on the forest floor, mocking the most manicured of lawns. Along the Art Loeb trail at more than a mile high, you'll have long-range views in all directions—and camping up here is cool even in the hottest months. Coming back down along the Big East Fork of the Pigeon River you'll find plenty of places to camp, hang out, fish, or just play in the stream.

Big East Fork (cont.)

Getting to the Trailhead

From the Blue Ridge Parkway at Wagon Road Gap, travel north on US 276 for 2.9 miles to the Big East Fork Trailhead on the left. Start from the lower lot.

GPS Coordinates

N 35° 21.96' W 82° 49.01'

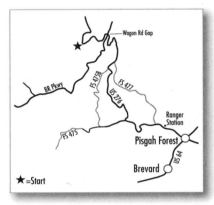

★=Start

Hiking Directions

Begin Walk past the info board and up Shining Creek Trail. You'll pass several well-worn campsites down by the creek on your left.

Mile 0.3 Turn right, away from the creek, heading uphill to continue on Shining Creek Trail.

Mile 0.7 Old Butt Knob Trail exits here on the right. Stay on Shining Creek Trail.

Mile 1.0 Reach Shining Creek. There is a small campsite here. Water is from the creek.

Mile 1.7 Pass another small campsite on the creek.

Mile 2.0 Pass a small stream waterfall on the right.

Mile 2.5 A steep, eroded side trail exits left downhill to a medium-sized campsite (5 to 6 tents) beside Shining Creek.

Mile 2.8 Pass another medium-sized campsite beside creek.

Mile 3.0 Pass a 15-foot waterfall on Shining Creek.

Mile 4.4 Step up onto Art Loeb Trail at Shining Rock Gap. You'll find campsites to your right. The spring that is the water source is 100 paces down Art Loeb Trail to your left. This is a great spot to spend the night nestled in a spruce-fir forest. Be sure to hike up to the shining rock on Old Butt Knob Trail. Continue the route by turning left on Art Loeb Trail.

Mile 4.8 Pass a second spring on your left.

Mile 5.1 Pass through Flower Gap, where the views are astounding.

Mile 5.7 The trails can be a bit confusing here. Make sure not to go over Grassy Cove Top. Instead, circle around to the left on Art Loeb Trail.

Mile 6.0 Look closely for a trail exiting left into blueberry and rhododendron bushes. Follow it to connect to Grassy Cove Trail.

Mile 6.1 Turn left on Grassy Cove Trail.

Mile 8.6 Cross Grassy Cove Prong just below a pretty sliding cascade. It's a great spot to take a break and cool your feet.

Depending on the water level, this may be a wet crossing.

Mile 9.0 It will feel like you've finally bottomed out when you reach the Big East Fork of the Pigeon River. There is a pleasant campsite here and another across the stream. If you're out for more than a night, this is a good last-night-out spot; there's plenty to explore. Look upstream on Grassy Cove Prong for a sizable waterfall. The route continues by fording Big East Fork and turning left on Big East Fork Trail. There are several small campsites along the river between here and the finish.

Mile 12.6 Reach the upper trailhead. Turn left on US 276.

Mile 12.7 Finish.

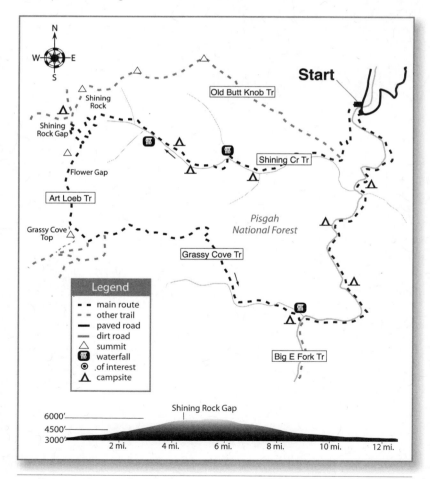

Flat Laurel Creek

Difficulty	Easier
Hike Distance	2.5 miles
Type of Hike	Loop
Total Ascent	400 ft
Land Manager	USFS
Fee	None

Some campsites halfway along this route have a view of Sam Knob.

Do you like wild blueberries? Make this overnight hike between mid-August and mid-September, and you can typically pick until you get tired of picking. Time it just right and you can have fresh blueberries in your breakfast oatmeal. The camping spots here are surrounded by blueberry bushes, so the distance from bush to bowl is a matter of feet. Fresh-picked doesn't get much fresher.

Maybe blueberries are just not your cup of tea, but you're looking for an easy hike and a cooling night out to beat the heat. No problem; this entire route is well over 5,000 feet. Frosts are not uncommon in June. It's also a great overnight to do with young backpackers. The short hike is not strenuous, Flat Laurel Creek is just the right size for splashing around in, and the open views are spectacular. Right about the time your kids ask, "How much farther?" you're there.

Getting to the Trailhead

On the Blue Ridge Parkway between US 276 and NC 281 near milepost 420, turn onto FS 816 and drive 1.3 miles to the trailhead parking lot at the end of the road.

Note: At times during the winter, the section of the Blue Ridge Parkway leading to the trailhead may be closed due to ice or snow.

GPS Coordinates

N 35° 19.53' W 82° 52.93'

Hiking Directions

Begin Walk onto Sam Knob Trail which is just to the right of the toilets.

Mile 0.6 Cross a delightful meadow surrounded by 6,000-foot peaks. A right turn here leads to the top of Little Sam, where the views are spectacular. You may want to set up camp on down the trail and return here later to make the side trip. The route continues, turning left on the trail leading down to Flat Laurel Creek. This next section is rooty and rocky.

Mile 1.0 As you reach the flats down near Flat Laurel Creek you'll find a number of nice campsites to choose from. Some are near the trail, others are spread out in the blueberry bushes. Water is from the adjacent stream. The route continues across the creek and turns left on Flat Laurel Creek Trail.

Mile 1.2 You'll pass a few more campsites along the creek; there is a pretty one in a birch grove. Water is from the adjacent stream. Just up ahead, Little Sam Trail exits right. Stay on Flat Laurel Creek Trail.

Mile 2.1 Right before crossing a tiny stream, you'll find a big campsite in a grove of balsam on the right. The water source for this site is the nearby tiny stream.

Mile 2.5 Finish.

Much of the hiking on this loop is wide open.

Flat Laurel Creek Map

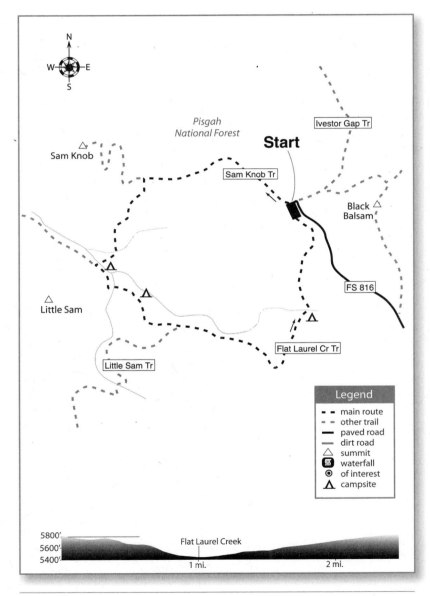

Pisgah National Forest

Ivestor Gap Tr

Start

Sam Knob Tr

Sam Knob

Black Balsam

FS 816

Little Sam

Flat Laurel Cr Tr

Little Sam Tr

Legend

- – main route
- – other trail
— paved road
— dirt road
△ summit
♨ waterfall
◎ of interest
▲ campsite

Flat Laurel Creek

5800'
5600'
5400'

1 mi.   2 mi.

Shining Rock Gap

Difficulty	Moderate
Hike Distance	9.3 miles
Type of Hike	Loop
Total Ascent	1,800 ft
Land Manager	USFS
Fee	None

Hiking up Black Balsam is thrilling, like walking on top of the world.

If there were a list of classic backpacking loops in the southern Appalachians, this would certainly be near the top of it. The high altitude, the panoramic views, the wildflowers, the wide-open terrain—it's all amazing. On some days the sun is so bright and the air is so clear you can't believe your good fortune. Other days clouds suddenly swoop in and blankets of mist swirl around you and your companions. You might forget you're in North Carolina and think you've been transported to the Scottish Highlands.

The loop starts with a bang, as you'll be standing atop Black Balsam Knob easily within the first hour of hiking. A mile later and you've summited another 6,000-footer, Tennent Mountain. Your destination for the night is Shining Rock Gap, deep in the Shining Rock Wilderness Area. If the sun is just right, you should be able to spot Shining Rock itself, sparkling in the distance as you head out towards the Gap.

On day two, an old rail grade, once used to haul out saw logs, brings you back to your car. It's pleasantly flat after the hills on day one.

Getting to the Trailhead

On the Blue Ridge Parkway between US 276 and NC 281 near milepost 420, turn onto FS 816 and drive 1.3 miles to the trailhead parking lot at the end of the road.

Note: At times during the winter the section of the Blue Ridge Parkway leading to the trailhead may be closed due to ice or snow.

GPS Coordinates
N 35° 19.53' W 82° 52.93'

Hiking Directions

Begin Walk out and around the gate on Ivestor Gap Trail. It's a rocky jeep road here. Just past the gate, look for Art Loeb Spur Trail on the right. Take it to climb up the mountain.

Mile 0.4 Turn left on Art Loeb Trail. Trails tend to head off in all directions here. The trail you want is the one leading most directly toward the summit.

Mile 0.7 Summit Black Balsam.

Mile 1.9 Summit Tennent Mountain.

Mile 2.6 Pass through a gap to continue on Art Loeb Trail.

Mile 3.0 Reach Ivestor Gap and the Shining Rock Wilderness boundary. You'll find camping spots back in the woods to your left just before the gap. Water is from a hard-to-find pipespring 100 yards or so down Graveyard Ridge Trail on the left, up in the bushes. Cross Ivestor Gap Trail and continue around the shoulder (not over the top) of Grassy Cove Top.

Mile 4.8 Reach Shining Rock Gap. The good campsites here are your best bet for the night out. Just before you get to the Gap, Shining Creek Trail enters from the left. The water source for the campsites at the Gap is downhill from the trail, 100 paces before Shining Creek Trail enters. If you want to see the Shining Rock, take Old Butt Knob Trail uphill from the Gap. Continuing on the route, turn hard back to the left on Ivestor Gap Trail. This old rail

Sunsets are always a hit at Shining Rock.

grade is mostly level all the way back to the trailhead.

Mile 5.2 Little East Fork Trail exits right. Stay on Ivestor Gap Trail.

Mile 7.4 Reach Ivestor Gap. You were here before. Bear right to stay on Ivestor Gap Trail.

Mile 9.3 Finish.

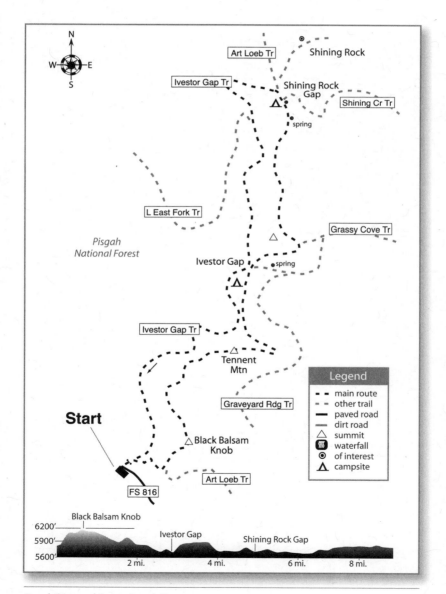

Graveyard Ridge

Difficulty	Strenuous
Hike Distance	13.3 miles
Type of Hike	Loop
Total Ascent	3,050 ft
Land Manager	USFS
Fee	None

Often you'll see local camp groups hiking over Black Balsam in the summer.

Wide open views, waterfalls, grass-filled woods, 6,000-foot peaks—that's just some of what you'll see and experience on this overnight trip. The route starts in a popular area. Unless you've picked an odd day, more than likely the parking lot at the trailhead and the sides of the road along FS 816 will be lined with cars. Folks are here to hike up to Black Balsam or out to Ivestor Gap. Most are just out for the day. You'll spot many more cars at the Graveyard Fields lot on the Blue Ridge Parkway. Surprisingly though, once you step onto the Mountains-to-Sea Trail, you'll leave the crowds behind. Finding a campsite is rarely a problem.

A variety of difficulties on this route contribute to its rating as strenuous. Footing on the MST is tricky. Rocks, washouts, and odd bridges over fragile marshy areas keep you on your toes. Route-finding can be a challenge in wilderness areas, and this is one example. You'll gain some serious altitude over relatively short distances. A full third of the route is very exposed. Sun, wind, and especially lightning during a summer storm can pose real problems.

Getting to the Trailhead

On the Blue Ridge Parkway between US 276 and NC 281 near milepost 420, turn onto FS 816 and drive 1.3 miles to the trailhead parking lot at the end of the road.

Note: At times during the winter the section of the Blue Ridge Parkway leading to the trailhead may be closed due to ice or snow.

GPS Coordinates
N 35° 19.53' W 82° 52.93'

★=Start

Hiking Directions

Begin Walk back up the road you just drove in on.

Mile 0.5 Turn left where Art Loeb Trail crosses the road. There are usually many cars parked here. As soon as you're off the road, bear right on the Mountains-to-Sea Trail.

Mile 2.0 Turn right on Graveyard Ridge Trail.

Mile 3.0 A couple of connector trails exit right, leading down to Yellowstone Prong. Stay on Graveyard Ridge Trail.

Mile 3.3 Turn right, back onto the MST.

Mile 3.7 Turn left here to stay on the MST. A right leads to Yellowstone Falls and the Graveyard Fields parking area on the Blue Ridge Parkway.

Mile 3.9 Pass through an area of campsites. These are good choices if you want to explore Graveyard Fields and its waterfalls.

Mile 5.2 Reach Skinny Dip Falls (Don't worry, most folks keep their clothes on). This is a good spot to take a break and, if it's warm enough, take a leap into the deep pool below the falls. Downstream of the falls and on the left side of the trail after crossing the creek is a large campsite that sees heavy use. There are better options farther along the route.

Lots of trails crisscross in the Graveyard Fields area.

Graveyard Ridge (cont.)

From the Art Loeb Trail the view is of ridges stacked on ridges.

Mile 5.5 Just before reaching the Blue Ridge Parkway, turn left to stay on the MST.

Mile 5.6 Turn left on Bridge Camp Gap Trail and head downhill.

Mile 6.1 Reach the river again. There is a nice campsite here.

Mile 6.8 There are campsites here on both sides of the river with the best one on the far side. If you're out for one night, this is a great place to spend it. To continue on the route, turn left and ford the river to head up Grassy Cove Trail which starts out steep, then climbs steadily for a couple of miles.

Mile 9.4 Bear left as a spur trail turns right to Art Loeb Trail.

Mile 10.0 Turn right on Graveyard Ridge Trail. You can see Ivestor Gap up ahead. As you head toward the gap, keep an eye out for a small stream passing under the road in a pipe. You may be able to hear it gurgling along. Just uphill on the right is a hidden pipe spring, the water source for the campsite at Ivestor Gap.

Mile 10.3 Reach Ivestor Gap. Turn left on Art Loeb Trail. You'll pass several camping spots just past the Gap. Water is available from the pipe spring.

Mile 10.6 Pass through another gap and then bear left to continue on Art Loeb Trail.

Mile 11.3 Summit Tennent Mountain.

Mile 12.5 Summit Black Balsam Knob.

Mile 12.8 Turn right on the Art Loeb Spur that leads down to the trailhead.

Mile 13.3 Finish.

Pisgah National Forest

Ivestor Gap Tr

Ivestor Gap

Grassy Cove Tr

Tennent Mtn

Big E Fork Tr

Art Loeb Tr

MST Graveyard Rdg Tr

Skinny Dip Falls

Graveyard Fields

Looking Glass Overlook

FS 816 Blue Ridge Pkwy

Start

Legend
- - - main route
- - - other trail
—— paved road
—— dirt road
△ summit
♨ waterfall
⊙ of interest
▲ campsite

6000'
4500'
3000'

Skinny Dip Falls

2 mi. 4 mi. 6 mi. 8 mi. 10 mi. 12 mi.

Spence Ridge

Difficulty	Moderate
Hike Distance	5.3 miles
Type of Hike	Out & Back
Total Ascent	1,300 ft
Land Manager	USFS
Fee	None

This is the only bridge that crosses the Linville River in the Wilderness Area.

Once you get down into the Linville Gorge, you'll see why such a short route is rated moderate; it's a rugged place. Trails are rocky, unmaintained, and never easy. That said, Spence Ridge Trail is the easiest way into the Gorge, leading down to a two-part log bridge over the Linville River. Once on the other side, the Linville Gorge Trail changes character. At times it's quite pleasant as it contours along just above the river. In other places, it climbs steeply up the gorge wall over rocks and roots where a missed step could spell disaster.

Don't let this description dissuade you from making this hike. Linville Gorge is a wonderful place. The river is beautiful, with boulder-strewn rapids and quiet pools. Cliffs ring the top of the gorge; you'll catch glimpses of them as you walk along. Campsites are plentiful, so finding a spot to set up a tent is rarely a problem. And the great thing is that with less mileage to cover, you'll have lots of time to enjoy the river. Whether you're here to fish, swim, or just hang out, you're bound to love it.

Getting to the Trailhead

From the village of Linville Falls at the intersection of US 221 and NC 183, go east on NC 183 for 4.5 miles. Turn right on NC 181 and travel 2.0 miles to turn right on Gingercake Road. Continue another 2.4 miles to a stop sign. Make a hard right turn on Tablerock Road. Continue 3.4 miles to the Spence Ridge trailhead on the right.

GPS Coordinates

N 35° 54.20' W 81° 52.73'

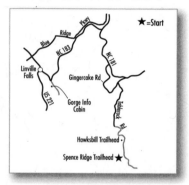

Hiking Directions

Begin Walk down Spence Ridge Trail and into Linville Gorge Wilderness.

Mile 0.4 Turn right to stay on Spence Ridge Trail, continuing downhill.

Mile 0.7 Pass a small campsite located on a small stream. Continue on down the trail.

Mile 1.0 A steep side trail leads down to a campsite beside a small stream.

Mile 1.5 Reach the bottom of the gorge and a two-part log footbridge over the Linville River. There's a huge swimming hole here with big boulders to hang out on. The trail continues across the bridge.

Mile 1.6 Turn left on Linville Gorge Trail.

Mile 1.7 A very steep side trail leads down to a well-used campsite on the river. Just across the river, a waterfall cascades into the gorge.

Mile 2.2 Reach several campsites, one on the river among some boulders, another above the trail a little farther along.

Mile 2.3 Conley Cove Trail exits to the right. Just beyond you'll find a well-worn campsite on the river.

Mile 2.4 Reach another campsite located right on the river.

Mile 2.6+ Reach a really big campsite on a flat area just up from the river. If the weather is warm, you'll enjoy the great swimming hole just below the campsite. The trail continues to follow the river with more campsites about a mile farther along. See the *Linville Gorge* route (p. 163) for locations. Otherwise, after your night out, return the way you came.

Mile 5.3 Finish.

Spence Ridge Map

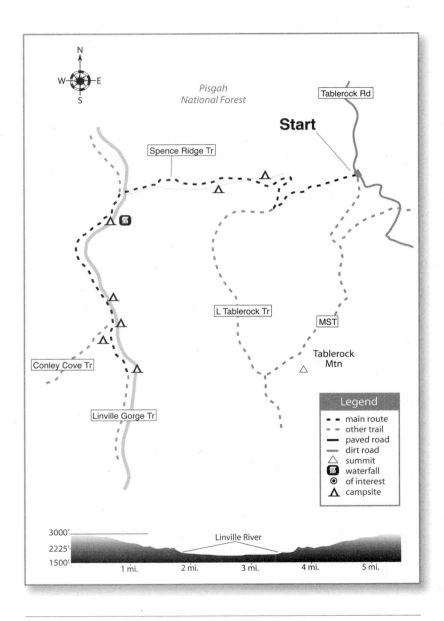

Pisgah
National Forest

Tablerock Rd

Start

Spence Ridge Tr

L Tablerock Tr

MST

Tablerock
Mtn

Conley Cove Tr

Linville Gorge Tr

Legend

- - main route
- - - other trail
── paved road
── dirt road
△ summit
▧ waterfall
⊙ of interest
▲ campsite

3000'
2225'
1500'

Linville River

1 mi.   2 mi.   3 mi.   4 mi.   5 mi.

Linville Gorge

Difficulty	Strenuous
Hike Distance	11.3 miles
Type of Hike	Loop
Total Ascent	3,560 ft
Land Manager	USFS
Fee	None

Hiking in Linville Gorge often means scrambling up steep rock outcrops.

Linville Gorge Wilderness is a very rugged place. Here the Linville River cuts a deep path where the only access is on foot (and, rarely, in boats by expert whitewater kayakers), down into a cliff-lined gorge of raw beauty. Trails here are tough. Getting down to the floor of the gorge means hiking extremely steep routes on trails that are barely maintained. Blowdowns are common, which means at times you'll need to crawl over tree trunks or beat your way through the bushes. Your knees will get sore, and likely you'll get scratched up a bit. And don't be surprised if you contract a case of poison ivy. Sounds like a wonderful place doesn't it? Actually, it really is—and it's a place you'll enjoy hiking into time and again.

This route takes you along the gorge's rim, through the area known as The Chimneys, then down the ultra-steep Chimbric Ridge Trail. Once along the river, camping opportunities are numerous, and the sites are large and well located. Linville Gorge Trail parallels the river, alternating between being right on the river and high above it on rocky slopes. You'll hike out on Spence Ridge Trail, the easiest trail in the wilderness area.

Linville Gorge (cont.)

Getting to the Trailhead

From the village of Linville Falls at the intersection of US 221 and NC 183, go east on NC 183 for 4.5 miles. Turn right on NC 181 and travel 2.0 miles to turn right on Gingercake Road. Continue another 2.4 miles to a stop sign. Make a hard right turn here on Tablerock Road. Continue 3.4 miles to Spence Ridge trailhead on the right.

GPS Coordinates
N 35° 54.20' W 81° 52.73'

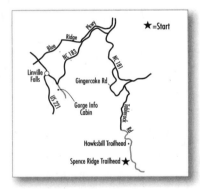

Hiking Directions

Begin Facing the Spence Ridge Trail as it heads into the wilderness area, go left on the unmarked trail that parallels Tablerock Road (FS 210).

Mile 0.4 Turn right on the Mountains-to-Sea Trail (white dot blaze).

Mile 1.1 A steep climb leads to this point, and from here a side trail leads to the top of Tablerock.

It's a steep 0.4 mile to the top. Continue on the MST.

Mile 1.2 Little Tablerock Trail exits to the right. Stay on the MST.

Mile 1.5 Cross through Tablerock Picnic Area and trailhead to continue on the MST. Just beyond the picnic area there is a large, well-used campsite. Frequented by climbing groups, this site does not have a water source nearby.

Mile 2.0+ Over the next few tenths of a mile you'll hike through The Chimneys.

Mile 3.5 Reach Chimney Gap. There are a couple of dry campsites in this region as well.

Mile 3.9 Near the top of the steep climb following the Gap and just before a small campsite, look for an unmarked trail heading right. This is Chimbric Ridge Trail. Follow it out a spine and begin a very steep descent into Linville Gorge. Expect it to be overgrown in places and with downed trees along the way. The next 1.4 miles is the most difficult section of the route.

Mile 5.3 Reach the bottom of the Gorge and Linville River. There are good camping spots here on both sides of the river, and if you are out for more than one night this is the best place to camp for the first one. The route continues, fording the Linville River and turning right on Linville Gorge Trail. This is a deep crossing and care should be taken during periods of high water.

Mile 5.6 Pinch In Trail exits to the left. Continue upstream on Linville Gorge Trail.

Mile 5.8 Reach a nice campsite right on the river.

Mile 6.3 You'll reach another small campsite just beyond a small stream crossing. A trail on the right leads to a larger site down on the river.

Mile 7.2 After traversing a fairly precarious stretch where the trail climbs high above river rapids through large boulders, you'll reach a high campsite. If you decide to camp here, you'll need to walk down to the river to get water.

Mile 7.8 Reach a nice campsite just above the river.

Mile 8.0 Another campsite, right on the river.

Mile 8.5 A large rock juts out into the river, forming a rapid with a fun swimming hole just below. It's a good spot to take a break. There is a small campsite here and a much larger one a short distance upstream next to another big swimming hole. This is a good option for those staying out just one night.

Mile 8.9 Reach another river campsite.

Mile 9.0 Just beyond a campsite, Conley Cove Trail exits up the hill to the left.

Mile 9.1 Here you'll find a campsite above the trail on your left and another one on the river among some rocks.

Mile 9.6 Down a very steep side trail is the last campsite you'll pass in the gorge on this route. It's pretty well worn but in an idyllic spot, just across the river from a small waterfall.

Mile 9.7 Turn right onto Spence Ridge Trail and walk down to cross the river on a log bridge. This is a great place to take a break before you climb up and out of the Gorge. It has a large swimming hole and huge boulders to hang out on.

Mile 10.3 Pass a campsite located down a steep side trail on a small creek.

Mile 10.5 Pass a small campsite on the left, on a small stream.

Mile 10.9 Turn left to remain on Spence Ridge Trail. Little Tablerock Trail enters here from the right.

Mile 11.3 Finish.

Linville Gorge Map

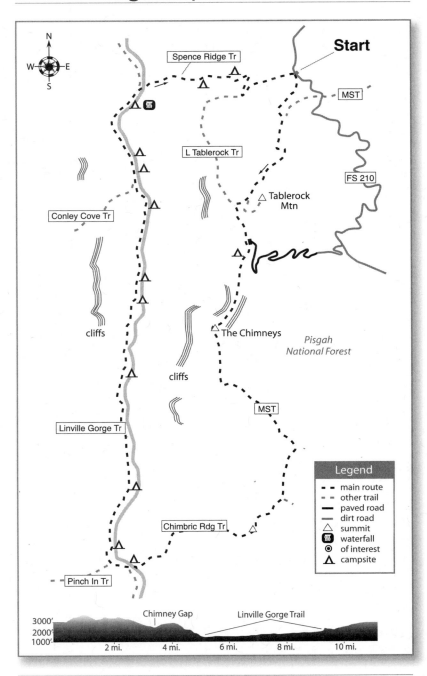

Start

Spence Ridge Tr

MST

L Tablerock Tr

FS 210

Conley Cove Tr

Tablerock Mtn

cliffs

The Chimneys

Pisgah National Forest

cliffs

MST

Linville Gorge Tr

Legend
- main route
-- other trail
— paved road
— dirt road
△ summit
🌊 waterfall
◉ of interest
▲ campsite

Chimbric Rdg Tr

Pinch In Tr

Chimney Gap   Linville Gorge Trail

3000'
2000'
1000'

2 mi.   4 mi.   6 mi.   8 mi.   10 mi.

Mount Mitchell State Park

Contact Information

Mt. Mitchell State Park
2388 State Highway 128
Burnsville, NC 28714
828-675-4611
www.ncparks.gov

Permit Required	Yes*
Fee	None
Max Group Size	None
Pets Allowed	Yes

*Free parking permit

Surrounded by the Pisgah National Forest and bordered by the Blue Ridge Parkway, Mt. Mitchell State Park is home to the highest mountain east of the Mississippi. Visiting Mt. Mitchell, at 6,684 feet is more like paying a visit to the wilds of Canada far to the north. Snow has been recorded on the summit every month of the year, and even in the heat of summer you can be guaranteed a cool night's sleep when overnight hiking from the trailheads there.

In the 2,000 acres that make up Mt. Mitchell State Park, there are eight trails to choose from. Some are completely within the boundaries of the park while others leave the park and head into Pisgah National Forest. The North Carolina Mountains-to-Sea Trail passes through the park as well, crossing the obvious high point before making a long descent to its Atlantic Ocean terminus over 700 miles away. Trailside camping is not allowed within the boundaries of Mt. Mitchell State Park. However, there are two established campsites in Pisgah National Forest just outside the park boundary. One is on Commissary Ridge, and the other is at Deep Gap. The hike out to Commissary Ridge is relatively easy, but the hike to Deep Gap is quite strenuous. At the trailheads you'll find self-service stations with information on how to complete and post your free parking permit. Note that the park gate opens at 8 am. During the summer it closes at 9 pm; in fall and spring it closes at 8 pm, and in winter it closes at 6 pm. You cannot enter or leave the park outside of these hours.

Commissary Ridge

Difficulty	Easier
Hike Distance	5.5 miles
Type of Hike	Loop
Total Ascent	1,258 ft
Land Manager	State Park
Fee	None

Grass growing in open woods gives this hike a western feel.

It's great when you can find a relatively easy hike that takes you over the highest summit on the East Coast; this one is real a champ. Hiking in the higher elevations is a very different experience than spending time lower down. It's like taking a trip to the Rockies or up into Canada. Everything is just different—the air seems clearer, it's certainly cooler, and the landscape takes on an alpine quality. Vast green meadows spread below the trees, inviting you to stop, lie back, and take a nap. The forest smells like Christmas trees, and you feel on top of the world.

This overnight takes you out to a beautiful campsite on Commissary Ridge below the summit of Mt. Mitchell. Located in a big grassy meadow, it's a pleasant place to spend the night. On day two, you'll climb right up to the top of Mt. Mitchell. The trail is a bit steep in a few places, but it's not too far to the top. Once there, be ready to feel like a hero. You'll stick out from the crowds with your trekking poles, boots, and backpack. Tourists will ask to take your picture and pepper you with questions about backpacking and sleeping out in a tent. Enjoy yourself.

Getting to the Trailhead

From the Blue Ridge Parkway east of Asheville, near milepost 355, take NC 128 into Mt. Mitchell State Park. Continue 2.5 miles to the trailhead at the park headquarters.

GPS Coordinates

N 35° 44.73' W 82° 16.65'

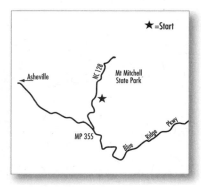

Hiking Directions

Begin Walk to the right side and around the back of the park headquarters building, around the gate, and onto Commissary Trail which follows an old roadbed.

Mile 1.2 Camp Alice Trail exits left here.

Mile 1.5 Buncombe Horse Trail enters from the right. This is also the Mountains-to-Sea Trail.

Mile 2.0 Reach the Commissary Ridge campsite. You are now in Pisgah National Forest. This is a beautiful site in a high, alpine-like meadow with room for several groups to spread out; it is the only campsite on this route. You'll find water 100 feet or so on down

the Mt. Mitchell Trail/MST. Get a good rest; tomorrow you'll climb to the top of Mt. Mitchell itself. The route continues by turning left here on Mt. Mitchell Trail/MST.

Mile 3.5 Turn left on the paved path leading to the Mt. Mitchell summit.

Mile 3.6 Reach summit of Mt. Mitchell. At 6,684 feet, it's the highest mountain east of the Mississippi. After enjoying the view and answering tourist questions, return down the paved trail past where you came in.

Mile 3.7 Turn left on Old Mitchell Trail.

Mile 3.9 Campground Spur Trail exits right; stay on Old Mitchell Trail.

Mile 4.1 Camp Alice Trail enters from the left. Bear right to stay on Old Mitchell Trail.

Mile 4.9 The trail passes right in front of the park restaurant here. You might want to stop in for a pot of tea or a bite to eat.

Mile 5.5 Finish.

Commissary Ridge Map

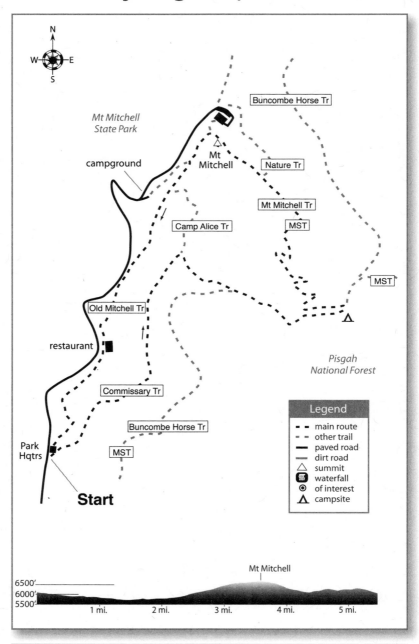

Mt Mitchell
State Park

campground

Buncombe Horse Tr

Mt
Mitchell

Nature Tr

Mt Mitchell Tr

MST

Camp Alice Tr

Old Mitchell Tr

restaurant

MST

Pisgah
National Forest

Commissary Tr

Buncombe Horse Tr

Park
Hqtrs

MST

Start

Legend

- - main route
- - other trail
— paved road
~ dirt road
△ summit
〰 waterfall
◉ of interest
▲ campsite

Mt Mitchell

6500'
6000'
5500'

1 mi.　2 mi.　3 mi.　4 mi.　5 mi.

Crest of the Blacks

Difficulty	Strenuous
Hike Distance	7.2 miles
Type of Hike	Out & Back
Total Ascent	2,650 ft
Land Manager	State Park
Fee	None

Like humps on a camel, the peaks along the crest are all above 6,000 feet.

Distance is certainly not the only factor in rating a route. This relatively short out-and-back overnight hike is very strenuous. In just over three miles you'll cross the tops of six of the highest mountains on the East Coast, and on day two, you'll do it all over again. All these peaks are well over 6,000 feet. This means your hike will be in an entirely different zone, one where the spruce-fir forest is dominant, the air is a bit thinner, and the weather is dramatically different. Clouds blow under you, above you, and sometimes, it feels like, right through you. In summer, thunderstorms can be sudden—and dangerous, as you are likely to be standing on the highest ground around, an invitation for lightning. Cool? Most definitely. Snow has been recorded in every month of the year.

The hike starts just below the summit of Mt. Mitchell and travels out a high ridgeline known as the Black Mountain Crest. Your destination is Deep Gap, a pretty spot over a mile high. At night you can see the twinkling lights of Spruce Pine in the distance. You'll return the way you came.

Crest of the Blacks (cont.)

Getting to the Trailhead

From the Blue Ridge Parkway, east of Asheville near milepost 355, take NC 128 into Mt. Mitchell State Park. The trailhead is at the Mt. Mitchell parking lot at the end of the road. Park in the lower lot; the trail starts at the picnic area.

GPS Coordinates

N 35° 46.03′ W 82° 15.86′

Hiking Directions

Begin Walk down the steps, past the picnic shelter, and onto the Deep Gap Trail (orange blaze).

Mile 0.9 Summit Mt. Craig (6,648 feet), a rocky bald with great views.

Mile 1.1 Summit Big Tom (6,581 feet). There are more great views here.

Mile 1.5 Big Tom Gap Trail exits steeply downhill to the right. Stay on Deep Gap Trail.

Mile 1.8 Summit Balsam Cone (6,596 feet) after a steep climb.

Mile 2.3 Summit Cattail Peak (6,584 feet) after another steep climb. You have left the park and are now in Pisgah National Forest, where the trail changes names to Black Mountain Crest Trail, though no sign marks the change.

Mile 2.8 Summit Potato Hill (6,475 feet) after yet another steep climb. This is the last summit before Deep Gap.

Mile 3.5 Reach the first campsite available on this hike. You are nearing Deep Gap. This site is farthest from the water source.

Mile 3.6 Reach Deep Gap. Here you'll find the only campsite with a water source on the entire Black Mountain Crest Trail. There is plenty of room for tents here with several small sites scattered around the area. For water, walk west down the old roadbed for a little over 100 paces. You'll see a tiny spring on the immediate left side of the road with a trench made by rocks leading out into the roadbed. After your night out, return the way you came.

Mile 7.2 Finish.

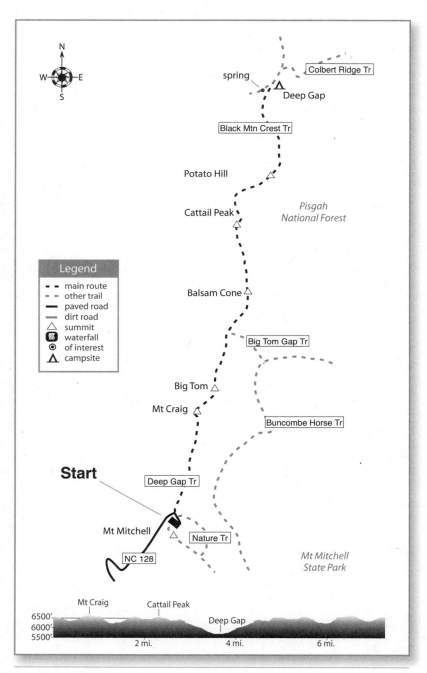

Montreat Wilderness

Contact Information

Montreat Conference Center
401 Assembly Dr
Montreat, NC 28757
800-572-2257
www.montreat.org

Permit Required	No
Fee	None
Max Group Size	None
Pets Allowed	Yes

Montreat Wilderness is located entirely on private land owned by Montreat Conference Center. The 4,000-acre conference center is affiliated with the Presbyterian Church, and 2,500 acres make up the wilderness, which is on the North Carolina Registry of Natural Heritage Areas. The rest of the acreage is taken up by the conference center, including houses and cottages, lodging establishments, meeting spaces, gift shops, recreational complexes, a campground, and worship areas. Some people live here year-round while others spend their vacations here or come to attend conferences. From a bird's-eye perspective, the area is shaped like a large bowl with the conference center in the bottom of the bowl while the trails traverse the sides and rim.

Inside Montreat Wilderness there are 21 trails totaling close to 30 miles in length. You'll find them to be well marked, well maintained, and easy to follow. Most are marked with colored, diamond-shaped plastic blazes attached to trees. The trails are open to the public and designated "hike at your own risk."

Overnight hikers will find two camping shelters/campsites in the wilderness area—one at Buck Gap and one near Walkers Knob. The hike on the following pages recommends spending the night at Walkers Knob.

The Seven Sisters

Difficulty	Strenuous
Hike Distance	13.4 miles
Type of Hike	Loop
Total Ascent	4,020 ft
Land Manager	Montreat
Fee	None

The Seven Sisters Ridge leads up to Graybeard Mountain.

Topping out on all seven of the Seven Sisters has long been a quest of many hikers in the region. On this overnight, not only will you visit each of the sisters, but their six brother peaks as well and the old man himself—Graybeard Mountain.

Seven Sisters Ridge is the local and most widely used name for a ridge of peaks rising increasingly higher above the town of Black Mountain. They can be clearly seen from I-40 and form half of a bowl around the Montreat Conference Center. On day one, you'll climb along the network of Conference Center trails, heading over the tops of the six peaks that make up the eastern ridge of the bowl. Be prepared for some steep sections of trail. Your home for the night is a shelter near the top of Walker Knob, with a great view looking over Montreat. On day two you'll climb to the summit of Graybeard Mountain (5,408 feet) before making the long descent across the tops of the Seven Sisters. It's a rugged stretch of trail (as a sign at the trail terminus clearly indicates), but no more so than many trails in the southern Appalachians.

Getting to the Trailhead

From I-40 at exit 64, take NC 9 north through the town of Black Mountain to Montreat Conference Center. Park at the trailhead on the right, immediately past the gate. A garden trail starts here as well.

GPS Coordinates

N 35° 38.32' W 82° 18.71'

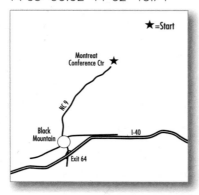

Hiking Directions

Begin Walk out of the parking area, cross the creek, and bear right onto Rainbow Mountain Trail (gray plastic diamond-shaped blaze). At the maintenance shed, bear right into the woods.

Mile 0.6 The trail gains altitude very quickly. At the split, bear right to go over Rainbow Mountain.

Mile 0.7 Gain the summit and continue over the top.

Mile 0.9 Turn right on Rainbow Road Trail (orange blaze).

Mile 1.2 The trail makes a Y; bear left to continue on Rainbow Road Trail.

Mile 1.3 At the next Y in the trail, you can go either way—they rejoin farther along.

Mile 1.4 At this intersection, Old Mitchell Toll Road exits to the right. Go left here on Old Trestle Road and turn right up the steps on Lookout Trail (yellow blaze). It is a very steep climb up to Lookout Rock. You'll go up over exposed rocks, roots, and wooden steps. Take your time.

Mile 1.6 Reach Lookout Rock for a fabulous view. Look across the Montreat Valley and you can trace the Seven Sisters. That's the ridge you'll descend on your second day. The trail continues up the ridge over Lookout Mountain, now on East Ridge Trail where you'll be following gray blazes.

Mile 1.8 Summit Boggs Bunion and turn left to continue on East Ridge Trail.

Mile 2.6 Reach Buck Gap. A little to your left is Buck Gap Shelter. Just to your right is the Old Mitchell Toll Road. Stay straight on East Ridge Trail.

Mile 2.8 Summit Brushy Mountain.

Mile 3.2 Reach Sourwood Gap. Cross over the road (Appalachian Way) to stay on East Ridge Trail.

Mile 3.7 Summit Rocky Head. Rocky Head Trail exits left. Stay straight on East Ridge Trail.

Mile 4.0 At Long Gap, turn left on Old Trestle Road Trail (white blaze).

Mile 4.7 At this point you are just below Pot Cove Gap. Continue on Old Trestle Road Trail to where you'll cross a small stream. Just beyond the stream, Graybeard Trail enters from the left. Continue straight as Graybeard Trail and Old Trestle Road Trail share the same track.

Mile 6.2 At this switchback, continue straight to view Graybeard Falls just up the trail, and then return to this spot and continue up Graybeard Trail.

Mile 7.0 At the creek, do not cross, but turn left to remain on Graybeard Trail. Old Trestle Road Trail continues straight here.

Mile 7.3 Reach Walker Knob Shelter. This is your home for the night. The shelter could easily hold 15 campers, and there is room for 4 or 5 tents out front. The water source for the shelter is the small stream you were following back down the trail a little way. After setting up camp, be sure to walk 0.1 mile out to Walker Knob for the view. The following mileage includes this side trip. On day two, continue up Graybeard Trail.

Mile 8.2 West Ridge Trail exits left here. Turn right to climb over Big Slaty (False Graybeard), the highest of the Seven Sisters, and head up to the summit of Graybeard Mountain.

Mile 8.4 Summit Graybeard Mountain. Soak in the views and then return to West Ridge Trail.

Mile 8.7 Arrive back at West Ridge Trail junction. Turn right on West Ridge Trail where you'll

gradually descend over the other six of the Seven Sisters.

Mile 10.9 Big Piney Ridge Trail exits left from the summit of Big Piney. Continue straight on West Ridge Trail.

Mile 12.6 Reach lower trailhead for West Ridge Trail. You are now in a neighborhood of mountain homes. The maze of streets leading down may seem intimidating, but hey, you just completed the Seven Sisters! It's easy compared to what you've just done. Turn right on Harway Lane. Follow it down to the stop sign to turn left on John Knox and then follow Louisiana Road down to Assembly Drive.

Mile 12.9 At Assembly Drive, turn right on the walking path that parallels the road.

Mile 13.4 Finish.

The Seven Sisters Map

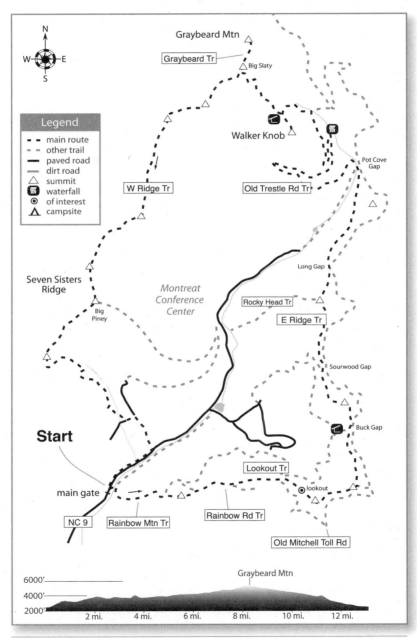

Legend
- **- -** main route
- ⋯ other trail
- ▬ paved road
- ▬ dirt road
- △ summit
- 〰 waterfall
- ⊙ of interest
- ▲ campsite

Graybeard Mtn

Graybeard Tr

Big Slaty

Walker Knob

Pot Cove Gap

W Ridge Tr

Old Trestle Rd Tr

Long Gap

Seven Sisters Ridge

Montreat Conference Center

Big Piney

Rocky Head Tr

E Ridge Tr

Sourwood Gap

Buck Gap

Start

Lookout Tr

main gate

lookout

NC 9

Rainbow Mtn Tr

Rainbow Rd Tr

Old Mitchell Toll Rd

Graybeard Mtn

6000'
4000'
2000'

2 mi.   4 mi.   6 mi.   8 mi.   10 mi.   12 mi.

South Carolina State Parks
& Mountain Bridge Wilderness

Contact Information

Caesars Head State Park
8155 Greer Hwy
Cleveland, SC 29635
864-836-6115
www.southcarolinaparks.com
(hikes pp. 183-190)

Permit Required	Yes
Fee	$12 ps pn
Max Group Size	Yes
Pets Allowed	Yes

ps = per site, pn = per night

Jones Gap State Park
303 Jones Gap Rd
Marietta, SC 29661
864-836-3647
www.southcarolinaparks.com
(hikes pp. 180-182)

Keowee-Toxaway State Park
108 Residence Dr
Sunset, SC 29685
864-868-2605
www.southcarolinaparks.com
(hikes pp. 191-193)

Mountain Bridge Wilderness comprises Jones Gap and Caesars Head State Parks. This 11,000-acre wilderness has over 50 miles of foot trails in a rugged area on the edge of the Blue Ridge Escarpment. You'll hike past towering waterfalls, along pristine streams, and beside sheer cliffs—and occasionally you'll hike up those cliffs. To get a camping permit, log onto the website listed above to reserve a campsite. The current website map leaves something to be desired. Not all campsites are listed, and it gives you only a vague idea of the actual location of each site. Still, it is handy because it is accessible 24/7. You can also reserve a campsite by phone and talk to a real person at the numbers listed above, or you can just take your chances and reserve a site at the visitor center when you arrive. Regardless of how you make your reservation, you must check in at one of the park offices, pick up your permit, and display it on your car while on the trail. No additional hiking permit is required.

At Keowee-Toxaway State Park, the same procedure applies.

Middle Saluda River

Difficulty	Easier
Hike Distance	1-5 miles
Type of Hike	Out & Back
Total Ascent	1,000 ft
Land Manager	State Park
Fee	$12 ps pn

pp=per site   pn=per night

Campsite #11 is located very close to Jones Gap Falls.

You can make this hike as short or as long as you want. Make it short by hiking just the half-mile to the first campsite on the Middle Saluda River from the Jones Gap trailhead. Make it five miles by hiking to campsite #13 farther upstream. Any way you do it, it won't be a difficult overnight trip, and the trail is wide and climbs very gradually as you head upstream. The idea here is to give yourself time to enjoy camping beside the river and exploring around once you've established your evening abode.

This is a great trip for first-timers. There's plenty to see (waterfalls, river boulders, wildflowers) and do (splash in the river, fish, just relax), and you can take your time setting up your tent and cooking your dinner on a tiny, lightweight stove. All things that come naturally to a seasoned veteran can be a bit of a challenge early on.

The route follows the beautiful Middle Saluda River upstream along what was once the Jones Gap Toll Road. There are six good campsites to choose from. Remember to check in with the ranger to get your overnight parking pass before hitting the trail.

Getting to the Trailhead

At 1.3 miles south of the NC/SC state line on US 25, turn west onto Gap Creek Road. Go 5.7 miles and turn right on River Falls Road. Continue another 2.1 miles to the trailhead at road's end.

GPS Coordinates
N 35° 07.51' W 82° 34.42'

Hiking Directions

Begin Walk out from the trailhead parking lot and cross the bridge onto a paved trail. After you cross a second bridge, Jones Gap Trail begins. It heads upstream along Middle Saluda River.

Mile 0.4 Rim of the Gap Trail exits left. Stay on Jones Gap Trail.

Mile 0.5 Reach campsite #8 with a 6-person limit. It's a nice big site right on the river.

Mile 0.7 Reach campsite #9 with a 6-person limit. This site has a big tent pad and is also right on the river.

Mile 1.0 A right turn here leads up Rainbow Falls Trail to Rainbow Falls. It's 3 miles round trip to the falls and back. Continue on Jones Gap Trail.

Mile 1.6 Reach campsite #10 with a 4-person limit. This site is situated in a nice spot near a bridge over the river.

Mile 1.7 Reach campsite #11 with a 4-person limit, situated on a level spot 50 yards from the river. This is the closest site to Jones Gap Falls.

Mile 1.8 Jones Gap Falls is right off the trail.

Mile 2.0 Reach campsite #12 with a four person limit. It has two levels and is on a hill close to the river.

Mile 2.5 Reach campsite #13 with a 6-person limit, which is right beside the river in a good location. This is the last campsite on the river. Should you continue upstream, you'd reach two more campsites at 3.5 and at 4.1 miles. Both are high above the river on knolls with drinking water a long walk away. For this overnight, #13 is the last best campsite. Return to the trailhead the way you came.

Mile 5.0 Finish.

Middle Saluda River Map

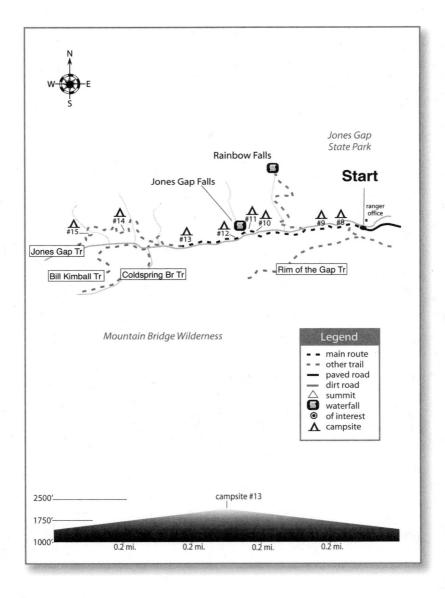

Naturaland

Difficulty	Strenuous
Hike Distance	10.2 miles
Type of Hike	Loop
Total Ascent	3,050 ft
Land Manager	State Park
Fee	$12 ps pn

pp=per site pn=per night

A suspension bridge crosses Matthews Creek just above the brink of Raven Cliff Falls.

When you look at the overall distance and the elevation profile, it's easy to think, "This can't be that strenuous a hike." Well, it is. The Mountain Bridge Wilderness, which comprises Caesars Head and Jones Gap State Parks, sits directly on the edge of the Blue Ridge Escarpment. Trails here tend to follow the tops of sheer cliffs or descend rocky stream gorges. This route does both, and the trails connecting the two can become pretty darn challenging when you're carrying a 20- to 30-pound backpack.

The hike starts out easy enough on a trail which heads out toward a viewing platform of Raven Cliff Falls and eventually down to a suspension footbridge near the very brink of the same waterfall. Here, cast out all ideas of what a normal trail is like. For the next mile, you'll climb down forest-covered Raven Cliff using ladders and rope handholds. Is it safe? Yes, but be careful, and allow yourself plenty of time.

There are several nice campsites to choose from along Matthews Creek. On day two you'll climb back up out of the gorge.

Naturaland (cont.)

Getting to the Trailhead

Caesars Head State Park is on US 276 roughly halfway between Brevard, NC, and Travelers Rest, SC, just below the South Carolina state line. From the park visitor center where you'll need to pick up your overnight parking pass, travel 1.2 miles north on US 276 to the Raven Cliff Falls trailhead.

GPS Coordinates

N 35° 06.95' W 82° 38.30'

Hiking Directions

Begin Walk across US 276 and onto Raven Cliff Falls Trail. It begins as wide as a road, but soon settles to a proper footpath.

Mile 1.4 Turn right on Gum Gap Trail. This is also the Foothills Trail (blue blaze).

Mile 1.7 Turn left to stay on Gum Gap Trail.

Mile 2.8 Turn left on Naturaland Trust Trail (pink blaze). Look for the "Falls" sign.

Mile 3.5 Cross Matthews Creek on a suspension bridge. Directly below you is a set of waterfalls. Look downstream and you see the brink of 420-foot Raven Cliff Falls. Once over the bridge, the trail character changes dramatically. You can expect ladders and handholds to get you through a cliffs section that drops down the same 420 feet Raven Cliff Falls—you can hear it off to your left. It's tricky going, so take your time.

Mile 3.8 Enter what is called The Cathedral, where you'll walk along the base of a high cliff with dripping waterfalls and hanging flowers and plants.

Mile 4.4 Reach Matthews Creek. Depending on the water level, you can either rockhop across or make use of an interesting set of parallel cables. The trail becomes less challenging once you cross the creek.

Mile 4.7 Dismal Trail exits to the left. Continue on Naturaland.

Mile 4.8 Reach campsite #D5, which is right on the creek and can accommodate up to 4 people.

Mile 4.9 Reach campsite #D4, which is also right on the creek. It can accommodate up to 4 folks on a slight slope.

Mile 5.3 Reach an unmarked campsite on the creek with a cable crossing to a much larger campsite on the other side. It's a pleasant spot.

Mile 5.7 Turn left to stay on Naturaland Trust Trail as an unmarked trail exits to the right.

Mile 5.9 Reach campsite #D3. This small campsite for a maximum of 4 people has no close water source, and campfires are prohibited here.

Mile 6.0 Reach the split-level campsite #D2, among some large boulders. The water source is a small stream over the ridge. The limit is 4 people.

Mile 7.1 Reach campsite #D1. This small site is for a maximum of 4 people. The water source is a tiny stream down the trail. It may go dry in the heat of summer.

Mile 7.2 Pinnacle Pass Trail exits here to the right. Turn left to remain on Naturaland Trust Trail.

Mile 7.7 Reach Rock Cliff Falls. This small waterfall slides down the cliff face and is a good place to replenish your water supply if you're getting low.

Mile 8.0 Reach US 276. You'll cross a driveway here and then parallel the road.

Mile 8.1 Cross US 276 to remain on Naturaland Trust Trail.

Mile 8.3 Turn left at the sign "Trail to Park Office." This is Frank Coggins Trail (purple blaze).

Mile 8.4 Turn right to stay on Frank Coggins Trail.

Mile 8.5 Cross the creek and turn left to stay on Frank Coggins Trail.

Mile 8.7 Turn right on Cold Spring Connector Trail (blue blaze).

Mile 9.1 Turn left on Cold Spring Branch Trail (orange blaze).

Mile 9.5 Bill Kimball Trail exits here to the right. Turn left to stay on Cold Spring Branch Trail.

Mile 10.1 Just before reaching US 276, turn right to stay on the Cold Spring Branch Trail.

Mile 10.2 Finish.

As you hike through "The Cathedral," the high cliff soars above you.

Naturaland Map

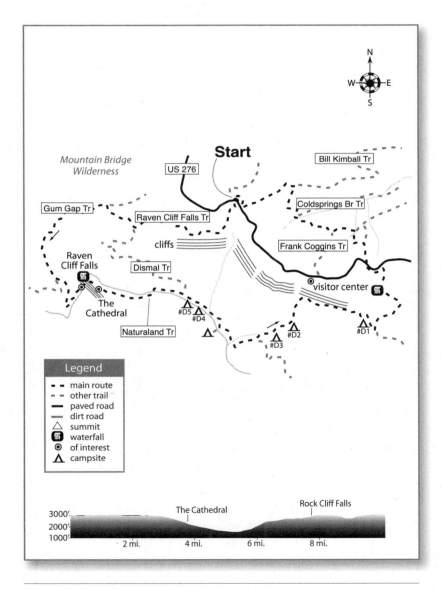

Pinnacle Pass

Difficulty	Strenuous
Hike Distance	18.6 miles
Type of Hike	Loop
Total Ascent	4,500 ft
Land Manager	State Park
Fee	$12 ps pn

pp=per site pn=per night

The clifftop view from Little Pinnacle Mountain is outstanding.

Forty-five hundred feet! That's a lot of climbing for South Carolina. That's a lot of climbing, period. The elevation gain on this route is 1,000 feet higher than the tallest mountain in the state. In the Mountain Bridge Wilderness on the Blue Ridge Escarpment, it seems like you're always going either up or down.

This overnight starts out fairly easy with a long stroll along the Middle Saluda River. This stretch has the best choice of campsites, though stopping overnight here means a short first day followed by a long second day. Still, if you want to camp next to the river, that's your choice. Once the route leaves the Middle Saluda, it takes you up and over Little Pinnacle Mountain on Pinnacle Pass Trail. There is one other campsite located about halfway along the loop, high on a ridge, a good walk from the nearest water source. Stay there and you'll spread the climbing over two days. Once over Little Pinnacle, drop down to Oil Camp Branch and then turn upstream for a climb that effectively lasts for the rest of the hike, through a botanically rich area and then up below the cliffs of Caesars Head.

Pinnacle Pass (cont.)

Getting to the Trailhead

Caesars Head State Park is on US 276 roughly halfway between Brevard, NC, and Travelers Rest, SC, just below the South Carolina state line. From the park visitor center where you'll need to pick up your overnight parking pass, travel 1.2 miles north on US 276 to the Raven Cliff Falls trailhead.

GPS Coordinates
N 35° 06.95' W 82° 38.30'

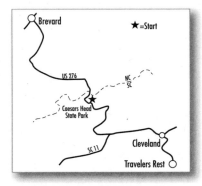

Hiking Directions

Begin Walk out the upper end of the parking lot and down Tom Miller Trail.

Mile 0.7 Turn right on Jones Gap Trail. Campsite #17 (maximum 4 people) is to your left on the banks of the Middle Saluda River.

Mile 1.0 Reach campsite #16 (maximum 4 people).

Mile 1.4 At the bottom of a switchback section known as The Winds, you'll reach a waterfall.

Mile 2.0 Reach campsite #15, a poor choice, on a spine well away from water.

Mile 2.6 Reach campsite #14, another poor choice on a spine, away from water.

Mile 3.5 Cold Spring Branch Trail enters from the right.

Mile 3.7 Reach campsite #13 (maximum 6 people), a nice spot right on the river.

Mile 4.2 Reach campsite #12 (maximum 4 people) on a hill above the river.

Mile 4.3 A side trail left leads a short distance to Jones Gap Falls.

Mile 4.5 Reach campsite #11 (maximum 4 people). Close to the waterfall, this site is on a level spot 50 yards from the river.

Mile 4.6 Reach campsite #10 (maximum 4 people) in a nice spot just before crossing a bridge over the river.

Mile 5.2 Rainbow Falls Trail exits left here. It's 3 miles round trip to view the falls. Continue on Jones Gap Trail.

Mile 5.4 Reach campsite #9, a big site with a tent pad (maximum 6 people), right on the river.

Mile 5.6 Reach campsite #8, a nice big site on the river (maximum 4 people).

Mile 5.8 Just ahead is the Jones Gap State Park trailhead. Turn right on Rim of the Gap Trail.

You'll walk for five miles along the Middle Saluda River.

Mile 6.1 Turn left on Pinnacle Pass Trail.

Mile 6.7 A very steep climb leads up to where you'll cross the top of a cliff face with views.

Mile 7.5 The trail levels for a bit and then goes straight up the spine of Little Pinnacle Mountain to this spectacular view spot.

Mile 9.1 A connector trail exits right, leading to Rim of the Gap Trail. Stay on Pinnacle Pass Trail. The stream here is the closest water source to campsite #P1.

Mile 9.4 Reach campsite #P1. (maximum 4 people).

Mile 9.9 John Sloan Trail exits right. Stay on Pinnacle Pass Trail.

Mile 12.4 A long downhill brings you to this spot, where

you'll turn right heading upstream along Camp Creek.

Mile 13.3 Mountain Bridge Passage Trail exits to the left.

Mile 15.0 Cross US 276 to remain on Pinnacle Pass Trail.

Mile 15.6 End of Pinnacle Pass Trail. Bear right on Naturaland Trust Trail.

Mile 16.2 Reach Rock Cliff Falls, a good place to take a break and get water if needed. You've been climbing for 4 miles and deserve it.

Mile 16.5 Cross US 276 to remain on Naturaland Trust Trail.

Mile 16.8 Turn left at sign "Trail to Park Office." This is Frank Coggins Trail (purple blaze).

Mile 16.9 Turn right to stay on Frank Coggins Trail.

Mile 17.0 Cross the creek and turn left to stay on Frank Coggins Trail.

Mile 17.2 Turn right on Cold Spring Connector Trail (blue blaze).

Mile 17.6 Turn left on Cold Spring Branch Trail, now following an orange blaze.

Mile 18.0 Bill Kimball Trail exits to the right. Turn left to stay on Cold Spring Branch Trail.

Mile 18.5 Just before reaching US 276, turn right to stay on the Cold Spring Branch Trail.

Mile 18.6 Finish.

Pinnacle Pass Map

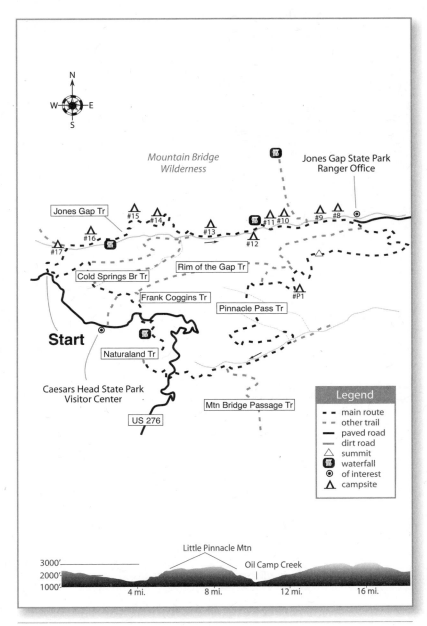

N
W — E
S

Mountain Bridge
Wilderness

Jones Gap State Park
Ranger Office

Jones Gap Tr

△ #15 △ #14 △ #16 △ #17

△ #13 △ #12

△ #11 △ #10 △ #9 △ #8

Cold Springs Br Tr

Rim of the Gap Tr

Frank Coggins Tr

△ #P1

Pinnacle Pass Tr

Start

Naturaland Tr

Caesars Head State Park
Visitor Center

Mtn Bridge Passage Tr

US 276

Legend
- **- -** main route
- **- -** other trail
- **——** paved road
- **——** dirt road
- △ summit
- ▓ waterfall
- ◎ of interest
- ⚠ campsite

Little Pinnacle Mtn

Oil Camp Creek

3000'
2000'
1000'

4 mi.   8 mi.   12 mi.   16 mi.

Raven Rock

Difficulty	Easier
Hike Distance	4 miles
Type of Hike	Loop
Total Ascent	900 ft
Land Manager	State Park
Fee	$12 ps pn

pp=per site pn=per night

From Raven Rock, you get a good view of Lake Keowee.

Though this is a short hike and rated easier, be aware that there are some short but steep ups and downs along the route. They are the kind that'll get your heart rate pumping and your lungs expanding. Other than that, the going is pretty straightforward and simple. The trail is clearly marked, the elevations are low, and there are just a few campsites to choose from, all basically in one spot.

Raven Rock is the only route in this book where you spend the night on a lake. With that comes some amenities; obviously there's no lack of water. If it's warm out, the swimming is great, and there's just something so pleasant about camping beside a lake. At night you can hear the quiet lapping of small waves on the shore. The croaking of frogs and other nocturnal noises carry well over water. In the early morning you might hear the whine of small outboard motors as fishermen head out to try their luck or folks talking on the golf course across the way.

As for hiking, you can look forward to crossing a natural stone bridge and the bluff at Raven Rock for views of the lake and mountains.

Raven Rock (cont.)

Getting to the Trailhead

From the intersection of SC 133 and SC 11 (20 miles north of Clemson), drive 0.1 mile west on SC 11 and turn right into Keowee-Toxaway State Natural Area at the camping sign. The trailhead is at the Meeting House information center.

GPS Coordinates

N 34° 55.96' W 82° 53.12'

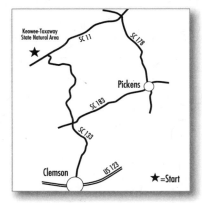

Hiking Directions

Begin Walk past the information kiosk and onto Natural Bridge Trail as it heads into the woods.

Mile 0.2 Bear right as the trail splits.

Mile 0.5 Cross the natural bridge, a large oblong boulder with a stream running underneath.

Mile 0.6 Turn right on Raven Rock Trail.

Mile 1.7 The trail goes both right and left here. You'll take the left route on the return. Go right,

and soon you'll start descending steeply to the lake.

Mile 1.9 Reach Raven Rock, a high bluff overlooking Lake Keowee with the mountains in the distance.

Mile 2.0 As you near the lake, you'll reach tent sites 1, 2, A, and 3, with #3 on a point almost at water level. Site #A is for groups, and #1 and #2 see the least use, since they are farthest (not much more than a stone's throw) from the lake. There is no stream nearby, so the lake is your water source. Don't forget to reserve your campsite ahead of time. After your night out, retrace your steps past Raven Rock.

Mile 2.6 Turn right to continue on the loop.

Mile 3.3 At the base of the steps, turn right across the creek and back onto Natural Bridge Trail.

Mile 3.7 At the top of the hill, reach the spot where Natural Bridge Trail splits. Turn right to continue to the trailhead.

Mile 4.0 Finish.

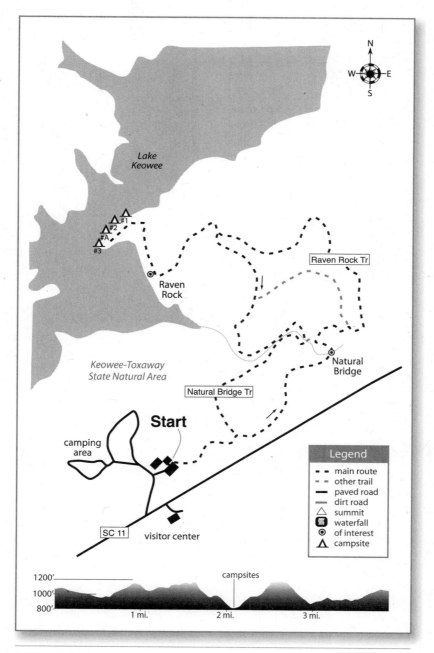

N
W · E
S

Lake
Keowee

△ #1
△ #2
△ #A
△ #3

⊙
Raven
Rock

Raven Rock Tr

Natural
Bridge

Keowee-Toxaway
State Natural Area

Natural Bridge Tr

Start

camping
area

Legend
- - - main route
- - - other trail
——— paved road
——— dirt road
△ summit
♨ waterfall
⊙ of interest
△ campsite

SC 11
visitor center

1200'
1000'
800'

campsites

1 mi.   2 mi.   3 mi.

Chattooga National Wild & Scenic River

Contact Information

Andrew Pickens
Ranger District
112 Andrew Pickens Cir
Mountain Rest, SC 29664
864-638-9568
www.fs.usda.gov/scnfs

Permit Required	No
Fee	None
Max Group Size	See below
Pets Allowed	Yes

The gem of South Carolina's Sumter National Forest is the Chattooga National Wild and Scenic River. This 57-mile stretch of whitewater is a site of exceptional beauty. The river drops over waterfalls, tumbles through gorges, races past huge boulders, and rolls sleepily past sandy beaches. Rafters, canoeists, and kayakers enjoy the lower stretches of river, while anglers like to test their luck and skill on the upper sections. Following much of the river's length is the Chattooga River Trail. This more than 40-mile trail begins at the US 76 bridge and travels north through Georgia before crossing to the South Carolina side and continuing to the Ellicott Rock Wilderness on the state line.

This book highlights the sections of the Chattooga River Trail that follow the river most closely. Hiking within sight of the river is a pleasant experience. You can take along a fishing rod and fish. In warmer months, you can swim in the pools below the rapids, then warm yourself on a sandy beach or a large flat boulder. In spring the wildflowers are amazing. Watching colored leaves swirl through the eddies in fall is meditative. And in winter, you're likely to have the place to yourself.

Along the river you'll find plenty of established campsites to choose from. There are also a few regulations to be aware of. Within the National Wild and Scenic Corridor, when possible, you should camp more than 50 feet from the river and/or the trail. Within the Ellicott Rock Wilderness (p. 204), group sizes should be limited to 12 people.

Pig Pen Falls

Difficulty	Easier
Hike Distance	3 miles
Type of Hike	Out & Back
Total Ascent	300 ft
Land Manager	USFS
Fee	None

There's a nice shallow pool below Pig Pen Falls for splashing around in.

This is a very simple overnight hike. It's good for families with small children. It's good for anyone on a first-time backpacking trip. It's good for waterfall enthusiasts. If you like to fish and would rather spend more time fishing than hiking, you'll like it. And it's good if you're just looking for a short hike into a really pleasant camping spot.

The route starts with the Foothills Trail at the end of Nichols Cove Road, one of many access points to the Chattooga National Wild and Scenic River. The Foothills Trail begins in nearby Oconee State Park, follows the border between South Carolina and North Carolina, and ends 76 miles later at Jones Gap State Park. But you're not going to hike anywhere near that far. On this route, the Foothills Trail takes you to Pig Pen Falls, where you'll pick up the Chattooga River Trail and hike down past Licklog Falls to the banks of the river. Along the way you'll pass a number of campsites beside the creek. If none of those suits your fancy, there is a final site on the river. With the creek, the two waterfalls, and the river itself, there's plenty to keep you occupied on this fun trip.

Pig Pen Falls (cont.)

Getting to the Trailhead

From Walhalla, SC, travel north on SC 28 for 8.1 miles and turn right on SC 107. Continue another 3.3 miles past Oconee State Park and turn left on Village Creek Road. Go 1.7 miles farther and turn right on Nicholson Ford Road. The trailhead is at the end of this road in another 2.2 miles.

GPS Coordinates

N 34° 55.51' W 83° 07.36'

★ =Start

Hiking Directions

Begin Walk out the back of the parking lot, past the information kiosk and onto Foothills Trail.

Mile 0.3 Reach a small campsite beside the creek. There is a larger one just over the footbridge.

Mile 0.6 Turn left on Chattooga River Trail. There are several campsites near this intersection as well, just to the right and beside the creek.

Mile 1.1 Reach Pig Pen Falls. If your destination is the Chattooga River, this is a great place to take a break before continuing on. The immediate area around Pig Pen Falls is designated no camping.

Mile 1.2 Off to the right of the trail you can hear Licklog Falls as it makes its plunge to the Chattooga. Every now and then you'll glimpse sections of it through the dense vegetation.

Mile 1.5 Take a short side trail on the right, down to this large campsite on the banks of the Chattooga River. There's room here for several tents, and it makes a good base from which to explore. You can walk upstream along the river to the base of Licklog Falls or just hang out at the campsite. Return to the trailhead the way you came in.

Mile 3.0 Finish.

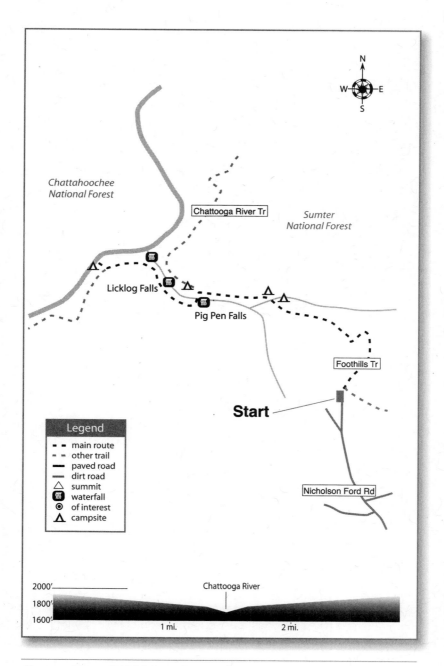

Chattahoochee
National Forest

Chattooga River Tr

Sumter
National Forest

Licklog Falls

Pig Pen Falls

Foothills Tr

Start

Nicholson Ford Rd

Legend
- main route
- other trail
- paved road
- dirt road
- △ summit
- waterfall
- ⊙ of interest
- ▲ campsite

2000'

Chattooga River

1800'
1600'

1 mi.   2 mi.

Chattooga National Wild & Scenic River

Chattooga River Trail

Difficulty	Moderate
Hike Distance	7-14 miles
Type of Hike	Out & Back
Total Ascent	2,800 ft
Land Manager	USFS
Fee	None

This section of the Chattooga River alternates big rapids with quiet pools.

River boulders, sandy beaches, waterfalls, great campsites. The Chattooga River Trail has all this and more as it follows the National Wild and Scenic Chattooga River for close to 40 miles on the border between South Carolina and Georgia. And like many streamside trails in the mountains, only occasionally does it hug the shore of the river. This is rugged terrain. Just as the river must carve out the gorge, the trail is carved into the slopes of the gorge, at times cutting corners to connect elbows and bends in the river.

You can spend one night out on this hike or as many as you like; this section of trail takes you along one of the least-traveled corridors of the river. Wherever the trail meets up with the river there is almost always a campsite or two to choose from. If you make it as far upstream as Big Bend Falls, you might want to scramble down and get a closer look at one of the biggest waterfalls on the entire river—a 30-foot drop. More than likely you'll find yourself lazing on a big rock by one of the many rapids or sunning on a sandy beach.

Getting to the Trailhead

From Walhalla, SC, travel north on SC 28 for 8.1 miles and turn right on SC 107. Drive 3.3 miles past Oconee State Park and turn left on Village Creek Road. Go 1.7 miles farther and turn right on Nicholson Ford Road. Continue another 2.2 miles to the trailhead.

GPS Coordinates
N 34° 55.51' W 83° 07.36'

Hiking Directions

Begin Walk out the back of the parking lot, past the information kiosk, and onto Foothills Trail.

Mile 0.3 Reach a small campsite beside the creek. There is a larger one just over the footbridge.

Mile 0.6 Turn right on Chattooga River Trail. There are several campsites near this intersection as well, just to the left and beside the creek.

Mile 0.8 Bear right as you reach the Chattooga River. The campsite here is the last one before the trail leaves the river for the next 2 miles.

Mile 3.1 Return to the river at a large pool below a big rapid. You'll find a campsite here.

Mile 3.4 Reach a large camp-site (room for 8 or 10 tents) right on the river.

Mile 5.6 The trail climbs high here. You can hear Big Bend Falls, a major waterfall on the Chattooga River, far below.

Mile 6.3 Big Bend Trail enters from the right.

Mile 6.6 The trail splits at a high-water detour sign. Go either way, depending on river water level.

Mile 6.7 Reach a pretty little campsite in a white pine grove. Water is from the river, and there is room for 1 or 2 tents.

Mile 7.2 When the water is low, there is a good beach campsite here with room for 1 or 2 tents.

Mile 7.3 Reach the last campsite (heading in this direction) for several miles. This is a good spot for 2 or 3 tents. There's a nice beach here as well as a large pool in the river. Return to the trailhead the way you came in.

Mile 14.6 Finish.

Chattooga River Trail Map

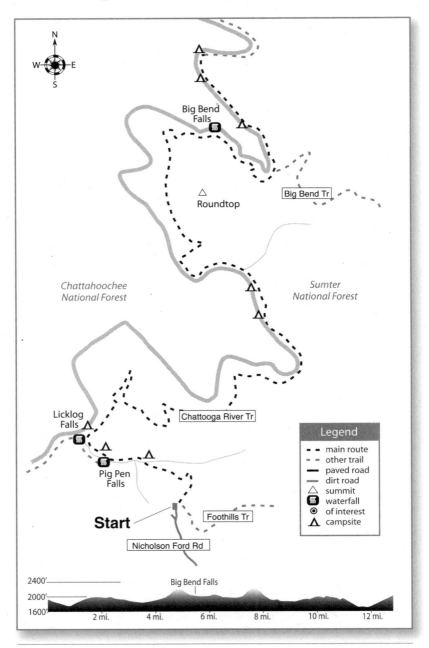

Big Bend
Falls

Roundtop

Big Bend Tr

Chattahoochee
National Forest

Sumter
National Forest

Licklog
Falls

Chattooga River Tr

Pig Pen
Falls

Start

Foothills Tr

Nicholson Ford Rd

Legend

- – – main route
- – – other trail
- —— paved road
- —— dirt road
- △ summit
- ⊞ waterfall
- ◉ of interest
- ▲ campsite

Big Bend Falls

2400'						
2000'						
1600'	2 mi.	4 mi.	6 mi.	8 mi.	10 mi.	12 mi.

Big Bend Trail

Difficulty	Easier
Hike Distance	7.2 miles
Type of Hike	Out & Back
Total Ascent	1,100 ft
Land Manager	USFS
Fee	None

In places the trail follows the banks of the Chattooga River.

Any time you get to hike along the Chattooga National Wild and Scenic River, it's a treat. The river corridor is both a natural and an official border between South Carolina and Georgia; it's one of the most rugged stretches of river in the southeastern United States. A hike into the gorge means you'll enter a pristine area where the waters run clear and the landscape is protected from development of any sort.

On this overnight trip, you'll walk out a less-used trail to a section of river known as Big Bend. One look at the map and it's easy to see how it got that name. You'll connect with Chattooga River Trail, which shares the tread with Foothills Trail here. Once on the CRT, you'll be walking upstream beside quiet pools and the occasional rapid. Large boulders jut into the river in places, creating big eddies with sandy beaches—good spots to relax or cool your feet or take a dip if it's warm enough. There are three good campsites to choose from; each is right on the river and all are ideal for a night out.

Big Bend Trail (cont.)

Getting to the Trailhead

From Walhalla, SC, travel north on SC 28 for 8.1 miles and turn right on SC 107. Continue another 8.2 miles to Cherry Hill Recreation Area. Park at the pullout on the east side of the road 0.1 mile south of the recreation area.

GPS Coordinates

N 34° 56.47′ W 83° 05.39′

Hiking Directions

Begin Walk across the road and onto Big Bend Trail.

Mile 1.7 Cross an old road/ trail. You'll see a fishing survey box on a black pole. Continue on Big Bend Trail.

Mile 2.2 Cross an old trail which heads straight down the hill. Continue on Big Bend Trail.

Mile 2.6 Junction with Chattooga River Trail. Turn right across a small bridge.

Mile 2.9 The trail splits at a high-water detour sign. Go either way, depending on river water level.

Mile 3.0 Reach a pretty little campsite in a white pine grove. Water is from the river, and there is room for 1 or 2 tents.

Mile 3.5 When the water is low, there is a good beach campsite here with room for 1 or 2 tents.

Mile 3.6 Reach the last campsite (heading this direction) for a good number of miles. This is a pleasant spot with room for 2 or 3 tents. There's a nice beach here and a large pool in the river. Return to the trailhead the way you came in.

Mile 7.2 Finish.

Big boulders jutting out into the river are good spots to take breaks.

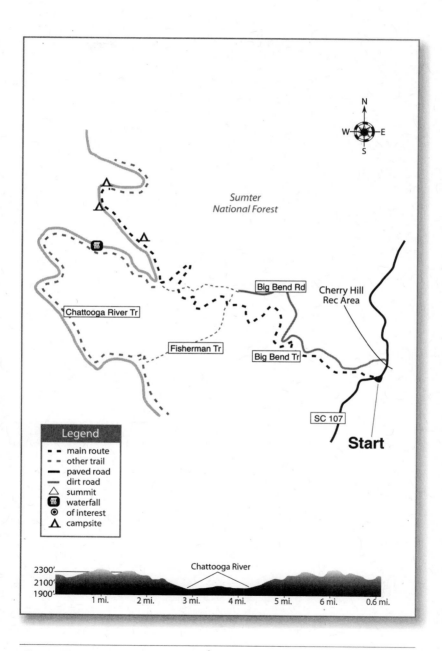

Legend
- - main route
- - other trail
— paved road
— dirt road
△ summit
▨ waterfall
◉ of interest
▲ campsite

Sumter
National Forest

Big Bend Rd

Cherry Hill
Rec Area

Chattooga River Tr

Fisherman Tr

Big Bend Tr

SC 107

Start

2300'
2100'
1900'

Chattooga River

1 mi.　2 mi.　3 mi.　4 mi.　5 mi.　6 mi.　0.6 mi.

Ellicott Rock Wilderness

Difficulty	Moderate
Hike Distance	18.8 miles
Type of Hike	Loop
Total Ascent	2,800 ft
Land Manager	USFS
Fee	None

Consider yourself lucky if you find Ellicott Rock itself.

Ever wanted to stand in three states at once? You can do that on this hike if you don't mind standing waist deep in the Chattooga River. Of course, it would still be a trick—unless you've got three legs.

Ellicott Rock Wilderness gets its name from an engraved rock, embedded somewhere in the bank of the Chattooga River, the border between North Carolina and South Carolina. It's fun to look for, but don't be discouraged if you don't find it; most people do not. This is still a great place for a backcountry overnight.

This route is rated moderate even though it is longer than many of the strenuous hikes in this book. The reason is that it just isn't that difficult. Still, you might want to spread it out over a couple of nights. There are plenty of campsites available, and you can spend more time enjoying the river section of the trail. It begins at Sloan Bridge Picnic Area near the state line and follows Foothills Trail for the first 7.6 miles. You'll then turn onto Chattooga River Trail and hike beside the river for a few miles before returning to close the loop on Fowler Mountain Trail.

Getting to the Trailhead

From Cashiers, NC, travel 9.2 miles on NC/SC 107 into South Carolina and park at Sloan Bridge Picnic Area. The trailhead is on the west side of the road.

GPS Coordinates
N 35° 00.21' W 83° 03.26'

Hiking Directions

Begin Walk out of the picnic area, southwest on Foothills Trail.

Mile 3.3 Cross Fish Hatchery Road to stay on Foothills Trail.

Mile 6.9 At this small stream crossing is a decent campsite with room for 4 to 5 tents.

Mile 7.6 Reach the Chattooga River. Turn right on Chattooga River Trail. There is a good campsite here with room for 6 to 8 tents.

Mile 8.3 A large riverside campsite is situated by a large pool with a sandy beach.

Mile 8.7 For the next 0.3 mile, pass through an area of very large campsites. Just up ahead cross a footbridge and then turn left as East Fork Trail enters from the right, soon passing another large campsite.

Mile 10.9 Just before reaching a state line sign, notice an unmarked but well-worn trail scrambling down the bank to the river. This leads to the site of Ellicott Rock and Commissioner's Rock, which mark the location where Georgia, South Carolina, and North Carolina meet. Commissioner's Rock is the easiest to locate. Chiseled into it are the latitude, year, and abbreviations for North Carolina and South Carolina. Ellicott Rock is inscribed simply "N G," presumably standing for North Carolina and Georgia. Good luck.

Mile 11.0 Reach a small campsite and a trails junction. You are now in North Carolina. This is a good campsite to use as a base if you want to explore and look for Ellicott Rock. Turn right on Ellicott Rock Trail and begin climbing Fowler Mountain.

Mile 12.2 Turn sharply back to the right on Fowler Mountain Trail.

Mile 13.5 Reach a small campsite here (2 to 3 tents). The water source is small stream.

Mile 16.5 Reach a small campsite on a small stream.

Mile 18.8 Turn right on SC 107 and walk 50 feet to finish.

Ellicott Rock Wilderness Map

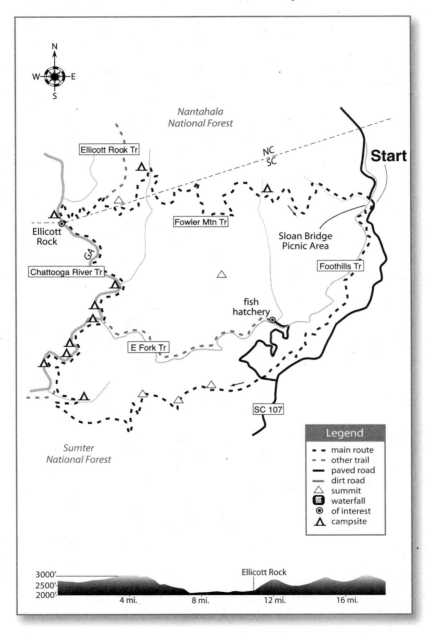

Start

Nantahala National Forest

Ellicott Rock Tr

NC / SC

Fowler Mtn Tr

Ellicott Rock

GA

Chattooga River Tr

Sloan Bridge Picnic Area

Foothills Tr

fish hatchery

E Fork Tr

SC 107

Sumter National Forest

Legend
- - - main route
- - - other trail
— paved road
— dirt road
△ summit
♨ waterfall
◉ of interest
▲ campsite

3000'
2500'
2000'

Ellicott Rock

4 mi.   8 mi.   12 mi.   16 mi.

Appendices

OVERLOOKING PISGAH DISTRICT FROM ART LOEB TRAIL

APPENDIX A—RESOURCES CONTACT INFORMATION

Great Smoky Mountains National Park (NPS)

107 Park Headquarters Rd
Gatlinburg, TN 37738
865-436-1200
www.nps.gov/grsm

Backcountry Reservations
www.smokiespermits.nps.gov
865-436-1297

Nantahala National Forest (USFS)

Cheoah Ranger District
1070 Massey Branch Rd
Robbinsville, NC 28771
828-479-6431
www.fs.usda.gov/nfsnc

Nantahala Ranger District
90 Sloan Rd
Franklin, NC 28734
828-524-6441
www.fs.usda.gov/nfsnc

Pisgah National Forest (USFS)

Appalachian Ranger District
PO Box 128
Burnsville, NC 28714
828-682-6146
www.fs.usda.gov/nfsnc

Grandfather Ranger District
109 E Lawing Dr
Nebo, NC 28761
828-652-2144
www.fs.usda.gov/nfsnc

Pisgah Ranger District
1600 Pisgah Hwy
Pisgah Forest, NC 28768
828-877-3265
www.fs.usda.gov/nfsnc

Sumter National Forest (USFS)

Andrew Pickens
Ranger District
112 Andrew Pickens Cir
Mountain Rest, SC 29664
864-638-9568
www.fs.usda.gov/scnfs

North Carolina State Parks

Gorges State Park
NC 281 South
PO Box 100
Sapphire, NC 28774
828-966-9099
www.ncparks.gov

Mt. Mitchell State Park
2388 State Hwy 128
Burnsville, NC 28714
828-675-4611
www.ncparks.gov

South Carolina State Parks

Caesars Head State Park
8155 Greer Hwy
Cleveland, SC 29635
864-836-6115
www.southcarolinaparks.com

Jones Gap State Park
303 Jones Gap Rd
Marietta, SC 29661
864-836-3647
www.southcarolinaparks.com

APPENDIX B—HIKE ROUTES ON THE APPALACHIAN TRAIL

APPENDIX C—HIKE ROUTES WITH WATERFALLS

APPENDIX D—HIKE ROUTES WITH NO HUNTING ALLOWED

Appendix E—Summit Bagging

What is summit bagging? It's when you hike to the top of as many high peaks as you can. Some people try for the highest in every state, or all those in the East above 6,000 feet. Others take it to extremes, for example, the highest on every continent—you get the idea. If you hike every route in this book, you'll bag a total of 45 summits, including Mt. Mitchell, the highest east of the Mississippi. North Carolina has 56 peaks over 6,000 feet; those listed in this book are shown in bold.

Milestone Press

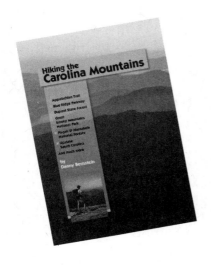

Hiking

- *Hiking the Carolina Mountains* by Danny Bernstein

- *Hiking North Carolina's Blue Ridge Mountains* by Danny Bernstein

- *Day Hiking the North Georgia Mountains* by Jim Parham

- *Waterfalls Hikes of Upstate South Carolina* by Thomas E. King

- *Waterfalls Hikes of North Georgia* by Jim Parham

- *Family Hikes in Upstate South Carolina* by Scott Lynch

- *Backpacking Overnights: NC Mountains–SC Upstate* by Jim Parham

- *Hiking Atlanta's Hidden Forests* by Jonah McDonald

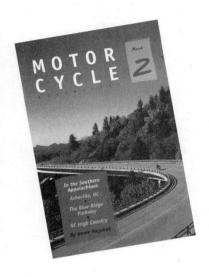

Motorcycle Adventure Series
by Hawk Hagebak

- *1–Southern Appalachians:
  North GA, East TN,
  Western NC*

- *2–Southern Appalachians:
  Asheville NC,
  Blue Ridge Parkway,
  NC High Country*

- *3–Central Appalachians:
  Virginia's Blue Ridge,
  Shenandoah Valley,
  West Virginia Highlands*

Off the Beaten Track
Mountain Bike Guide Series
by Jim Parham

- *Vol. 1: WNC–Smokies*
- *Vol. 2: WNC–Pisgah*
- *Vol. 3: N. Georgia*
- *Vol. 4: E. Tennessee*
- *Vol. 5: N. Virginia*

Milestone Press

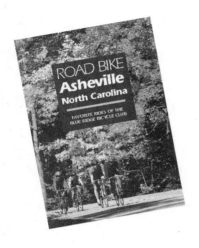

Road Bike Guide Series

- *Road Bike Asheville, NC: Favorite Rides of the Blue Ridge Bicycle Club* by The Blue Ridge Bicycle Club

- *Road Bike North Georgia: 25 Great Rides in the Mountains and Valleys of North Georgia* by Jim Parham

- *Road Bike the Smokies* by Jim Parham

Family Adventure

- *Natural Adventures in the Mountains of North Georgia* by Mary Ellen Hammond & Jim Parham

- *Family Hikes in Upstate South Carolina* by Scott Lynch

Rockhounding

- *A Rockhounding Guide
  to North Carolina's Blue
  Ridge Mountains*
  by Michael Streeter

Can't find the Milestone Press book you want at a bookseller near you?
Don't despair—you can order it directly from us. Call us at
828-488-6601 or shop online at www.milestonepress.com.

Great Hikes
of the Southern Appalachians

Put the hikes from this book on your phone.

iPhone or Android

Taking a hike doesn't get much easier! With hundreds of routes to choose from in Western North Carolina, Upstate South Carolina, North Georgia, and metro Atlanta, this mobile app helps you search and select a hike, get to the trailhead, and find your way on the trail. All hikes are adapted from Milestone Press's best guidebooks, so you know they're created by expert hikers and tested by countless users. Watch for updates as more routes are added to the list! Once you've purchased and installed the GPS-enabled hikes on your phone, all your trail information is fully functional, with no wi-fi or data connection required.

All your favorite hikes from this and other Milestone Press guidebooks are now accessible on your smart phone.

- Hundreds of hikes to choose from in the mountains of North and South Carolina and Georgia, as well as the Atlanta metro area

- GPS-enabled so you always know precisely where you are on the trail and en route to the trailhead

- Look for **Great Hikes of the Southern Appalachians** at the Apple App or Google Play store.

- Downloading the app is easy. Just scan the QR code with your iPhone or android for direct access to **Great Hikes**.

An App for iPhone or Android